Using Performance Improvement Tools

In Health Care Settings

Joint Commission Mission

The mission of the Joint Commission on Accreditation of Healthcare Organizations is to improve the quality of care provided to the public through the provision of health care accreditation and related services that support performance improvement in health care organizations.

Joint Commission educational programs and publications support, but are separate from, the accreditation activities of the Joint Commission. Attendees at Joint Commission educational programs and purchasers of Joint Commisssion publications receive no special consideration or treatment in, or confidential information about, the accreditation process

Printed in the U.S.A. 5 4 3 2 1

Requests for permission to reprint or make copies of any part of this book should be addressed to:

Permissions Editor
Department of Publications
Joint Commission on Accreditation of Healthcare Organizations
One Renaissance Boulevard
Oakbrook Terrace, IL 60181

ISBN: 0-86688-489-0

Library of Congress Catalog Number: 96-076180

Contents

Section 1 Performance Improvement in Health Care

More than ever, hospitals and other health care organizations are challenged to provide high-quality, cost-effective care and to document and continuously improve that care. As providers compete for a piece of the limited health care economic pie, they must demonstrate to payers, purchasers, and consumers that they provide coordinated, efficient care that results in desirable outcomes, including not just improved health but patient satisfaction as well.

A number of related factors contribute to this focus on quality and efficiency, including the following:

- The growth of managed care and capitation payment is making hospitals a cost center rather than a revenue center.
- Hospitals are joining or forming integrated delivery systems and other partnerships to enhance their ability to provide a continuum of care to consumers in a defined geographic region and to compete for managed care contracts.
- Payers, purchasers, and consumers are demanding information on the efficiency and quality of providers.

These challenges have made high-quality, efficient health care not just a laudable ambition but an operational necessity.

Accompanying this mandate for quality and efficiency has been an increased understanding of how these goals can be achieved. Implementation of continuous quality improvement, total quality management, outcomes management, reengineering, and other approaches to performance improvement have provided health care providers an enhanced understanding of how they provide care, why unwanted variation in processes and outcomes exists, and how to improve those processes and outcomes.

Although some improvement approaches, such as reengineering, are widely associated with the push to control costs, all the approaches mentioned here are forms of quality improvement; that is, whether their goal is to enhance efficiency or patient outcomes, they contribute to the overall quality and value of an organization's performance.

Among the most important contributions of these efforts is an array of tools to help health care professionals to

- set priorities and otherwise plan for improvement;
- work effectively in teams to improve processes;
- understand the organization's processes; and
- select and implement actions to improve processes and their outcomes.

This book introduces many of these tools and shows how health care professionals can use them.

To provide a context for these tools, this chapter discusses some core concepts of performance improvement shared by various approaches to improvement. Next, it introduces some methods for improvement within which these tools can be used. Finally, it offers an overview of various tools used in performance improvement. Subsequent chapters contain more detailed descriptions of the tools and how they are used, along with examples. Finally, the book presents one case study and one exercise that show readers how the tools can be used as part of a coordinated, successful effort to improve performance.

The Importance of Performance Improvement

The changing health care system has further spotlighted the *performance* of health care providers. Health care purchasers and payers are demanding that providers document their provision of efficient, high-quality care. Consumers, also, are more vocal about their need for information about health care providers' performance. Measures such as cost per health plan member per month, functional health status after treatment, and patient satisfaction are becoming more common tools for communicating the quality of performance to payers, purchasers, and the public. Purchasers and payers are looking for evidence that hospitals and other health care organizations manage their costs well, satisfy their customers, and have desirable outcomes. Consumers, also, more often look to hospitals for evidence that they serve their patients well.

External groups, however, are not the only ones seeking information about the performance of health care providers. Provider organizations themselves are seeking this information in an effort to continuously understand and improve their performance. From the provider's perspective, continuous improvement is an imperative not only to fulfill their missions to provide high-quality care to their patients and communities, but also to survive in an increasingly competitive market.

The effort to measure, assess, and improve health care performance got a needed jump-start in the mid-1980s from an unexpected source. American industry, spurred by competition from overseas, had begun using a new approach to improvement. Rather than focusing on inspection—one traditional means of "assuring" quality—this approach focused on "doing right things right the first time." In other words, business executives sought to understand the *processes* that their organizations used and to continuously improve the design of those processes.

This approach is widely attributed to W. Edwards Deming and to the Japanese companies that adopted his philosophy as a day-to-day way of doing business.

The concept of continuously improving processes has a number of important implications:

- Leadership commitment to continuous improvement—in the form of necessary resources and active involvement—is essential if the effort is to succeed.
- Most opportunities for improvement arise not by identifying individuals who are performing badly, but by identifying and correcting problems with the processes within which individuals must work.
- Many work process problems arise from handoffs of projects between people or departments.
- Organizations must listen to their customers—both internal and external—and fulfill their needs and expectations.
- Reliable measurement and accurate assessment are necessary to understand current performance and to target areas for improvement.
- A systematic improvement method is necessary to guide measurement, assessment, and improvement.

In the mid-1980s, a number of health care organizations began using this approach to improvement. Long frustrated by improvement efforts that seemed ineffective, seemed to target individuals, and seemed to be carried out only to satisfy regulators and accreditors, health care leaders were looking for a way to create meaningful improvement in clinical outcomes as well as to improve financial performance in the face of an intense need to manage costs. Many health care leaders embraced the idea that multidisciplinary teams of "customers" and "suppliers" could work together to understand current performance and to improve processes as a way to improve performance.

Today, different improvement concepts seem to crop up weekly in health care literature. Benchmarking, reengineering, outcomes management, and critical paths are just some of the concepts being applied in health care. Organizations are working to develop standardized measures of health care quality, and information systems companies are designing systems to aid in performance measurement and assessment. Given the demands in the current climate for high quality and efficiency, the quest for knowledge about performance improvement should continue to intensify.

Performance Improvement Methods

An organization may label its approach to improvement "continuous quality improvement" or "total quality management"; an organization's approach to improvement may involve highly computerized data collection and analysis or manual check sheets and run charts drawn on graph paper. No matter the name or level of sophistication, a successful approach to improvement requires a systematic method—one that guides people through the stages of improvement to help ensure that improvement actions are based on sound data and analysis and that the actions attain the desired results.

Many such methods have been developed. Perhaps the most famous is the Plan-Do-Study-Act (PDSA) cycle (see Figure 1-1, page 5). This cycle, which is also called Plan-Do-Check-Act or the Shewhart cycle, was created by Walter Shewhart, a scientist who helped craft modern quality control and an understanding of process variation. The cycle was taught by quality guru Deming. *Plan* refers to first understanding the process, then proposing an improvement, and finally deciding how an improvement action will be tested and how data will be collected to determine what effect the action has. *Do* means to perform the test by implementing the action on a small scale. *Study* involves analyzing the effect of the action being tested. *Act* means to fully implement the action or reassess the improvement action taken and perhaps then choose another action. The cycle is continuous and can be entered at any point.

Another well-known process, FOCUS-PDCA®, was developed by the Hospital Corporation of America (now part of Columbia Health Care Corporation). FOCUS stands for

- **F**ind a process to improve,
- **O**rganize a team that knows the process,
- **C**larify current knowledge of the process,
- **U**nderstand causes of process variation, and
- **S**elect the process improvement.

These steps lead to the PDCA cycle, which is used to test and imple-

Plan-Do-Study-Act (PDSA) Cycle

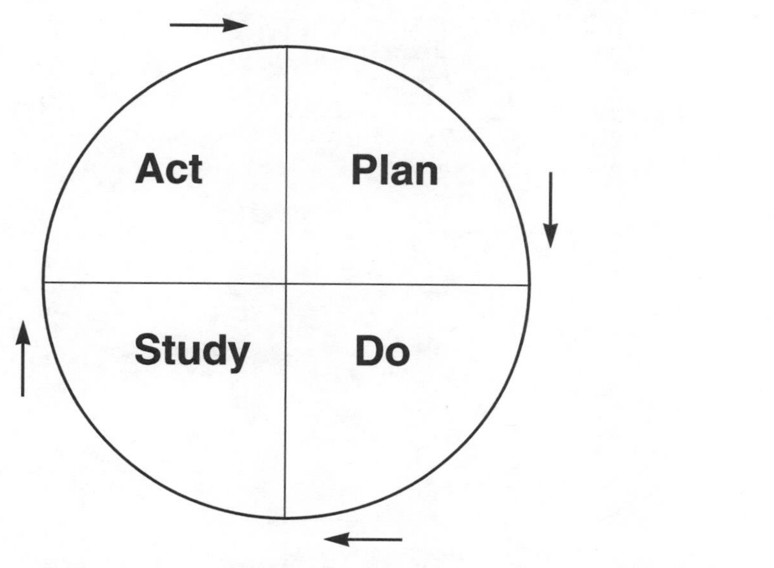

Figure 1-1 *The PDSA cycle—also called the Shewart cycle—is useful in planning, testing, assessing, and implementing an action to improve a process.*

ment the process improvement.

To help health care professionals understand the steps of performance improvement—steps that most improvement processes share—the Joint Commission has developed a *cycle for improving performance*. The cycle, illustrated in Figure 1-2 (page 6), integrates a number of different approaches to performance improvement. It presents the basic stages of performance improvement in a flexible format that is easy to incorporate into the day-to-day operations of an organization, yet sophisticated enough to apply to complex, long-term projects.

The cycle consists of four key activities—*design*, *measure*, *assess*, and *improve*—and a series of major inputs and outputs related to these key activities. In general, these activities—and their inputs and outputs—help an organization create effective new processes, study current processes, and improve current processes in order to help the organization meet its goals and serve its customers.

Design

Designing new services (and the processes that make up those services) and redesigning existing services to increase efficiency and improve outcomes are ongoing activities for health care organizations. Examples of design run the gamut from opening a branch in a new community to creating an intake and referral process for a new clinical service to

Cycle for Improving Performance

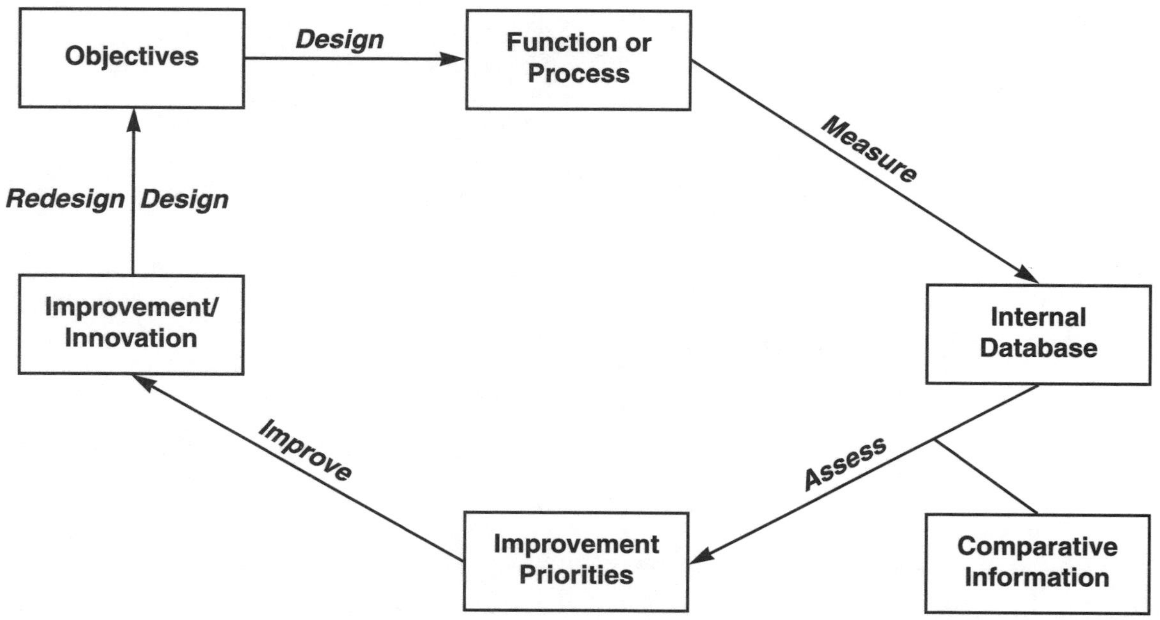

Figure 1-2 *This cycle represents the basic activities (shown by the arrows) involved in improving performance, as well as the input to and outputs from those activities (shown by the boxes). The cycle can be entered at any point.*

implementing a new information system. The design stage in the cycle for improving performance involves identifying the objectives for a process, and then creating a design that meets those objectives.

Clear objectives are necessary to focus the design effort on achieving a specific goal or purpose. In defining these objectives, organization staff and leaders should consider the overall mission, vision, and strategic plan of the organization, and then determine how the process in question fits into them. The following key factors should be considered:

- How the process affects patients, staff, and other important groups;
- What expertise and experience within the organization may apply to designing the process;
- What expertise and experience outside the organization may be tapped in the design effort;
- What data are necessary to design the process and how the data will be collected and analyzed; and
- What resources are available and what funds, staff time, equipment, and other resources are required.

To help ensure success, a team that will design a process should include representatives from all groups involved in the process; gather expertise from within and outside the organization; and use a systematic method to determine the process's effect on matters such as patient outcomes, organizational resources, and organizational competitiveness. In designing the process, the team must be sure to base decisions and activities on valid, reliable data and also keep in mind that the most successful processes will achieve the organization's objectives by facilitating effectiveness and efficiency in customer-supplier relationships.

Designing a new process involves planning, teamwork, data collection, data analysis, and understanding of root causes of performance. Therefore, all the tools described in this book can apply to a design effort.

Measure

The goal of measurement is to collect valid, reliable data that will be used to assess how well a process is working and where specific improvement may be needed. Ongoing measurement results in an organization-specific database that contains information about performance, outcomes, satisfaction, cost, and judgments about quality and value.

Measurement is based on indicators, which are explained in more detail in Section 4 (pages 67–72) of this book. Essentially, indicators are valid and reliable quantitative process or outcome measures that articulate the specific information to be collected. Indicators generally are related to one or more of the dimensions of performance, which are efficacy, appropriateness, availability, timeliness, effectiveness, continuity, safety, efficiency, and respect and caring.

When deciding what to measure, consider which patient care functions and organizational functions are of highest priority. Functions and processes that affect the greatest number of people, that are high risk, or that are problem prone are good candidates for ongoing measurement or measurement as part of a specific improvement effort.

In addition to providing baseline data when an improvement effort is launched, measurement will help demonstrate the effect of improvement actions when those actions are tested and after they have been fully implemented. Measurement also is necessary to determine whether key processes are statistically "in control." Once a process is statistically in control and is stabilized at an acceptable range of performance, measures may be taken periodically to verify that improved performance is sustained.

Assess

Assessment involves translating data collected during measurement into information that can be used to draw conclusions about performance and to improve processes.

One form of assessment is comparing current performance with historical patterns of performance within the organization. However, to better understand performance levels, assessment should also look outside the organization for sources to use for objective comparison. For example, health care associations, payers, and state and federal governments all aggregate information about performance and cost. Another method of comparing performance is benchmarking, which is predicated on in-depth study of how other organizations routinely perform key processes and consistently achieve good outcomes.

Also, professional societies and expert panels routinely develop scientifically based descriptions of patient care processes. These are good sources of "best practices" for a given procedure or treatment. Assessing variation from such established procedures is another good way to identify opportunities for improvement.

It also is important to examine not only the outcomes but also the causes of current performance. This knowledge is gained through in-depth analysis of a process and requires identification of a process's steps and decision points; the various people, actions, and equipment associated with the process; and the causes of variation in performance.

Assessment should identify opportunities for improvement and set priorities for improvement. Because a significant investment of time and effort is sometimes needed to improve processes, the organization's mission, strategic plans, resources, and other such issues should be considered when setting improvement priorities.

Tools such as control charts, flowcharts, cause-and-effect diagrams and Pareto charts—all described in this book—help in identifying variation in a process, understanding how a process performs, and determining the root causes for performance.

Improve

Improvement actions are based on the results of measurement and assessment. To improve a process, a team creates, tests, and implements specific innovations, which may involve a redesign of the process or the design of a new process. A standard yet flexible improvement method will help ensure that actions address root causes, involve the right people, and result in desired and sustained changes.

In general, an improvement effort will involve

- selecting an improvement action, which often involves redesigning a process;
- determining who will implement the action;
- determining how the action will be implemented;
- determining how data will be collected to measure the action's effect;

- implementing the action on a small scale or for a limited time;
- assessing the effectiveness of the action; and
- implementing the action fully, if the results of the test warrant it.

Many of the tools in this book can be used in the improve phase of the cycle. Planning tools such as critical paths can be used to redesign processes. Teamwork tools such as brainstorming and multivoting can be used to select an improvement action. Other teamwork tools such as storyboards can be used to document the improvement activities. Data-collection tools such as check sheets can be used to measure the improvement. Analysis tools such as control charts can be used to determine whether the action has had the desired effect.

Using the Cycle for Improving Performance

The cycle for improving performance is an effective tool for creating successful processes. When the process or function being addressed crosses departmental lines, a special team may need to be assembled, but one of the merits of this cycle is that it can easily be carried out by work groups as part of everyday activities. It was designed for seamless use with the daily functions and processes of the organization, and it has an application that goes beyond specific performance improvement projects.

Like any improvement method, the cycle for improving performance will not succeed without leadership commitment, planning, and oversight, as well as information management to facilitate the capture, extraction, and organization of data.*

Performance Improvement Tools and Techniques

In addition to a systematic performance improvement method, effective tools are necessary to design, measure, assess, and improve performance. Without the proper tools, performance improvement efforts are left to trial and error, and the results may be not only disappointing but costly.

The purpose of this book is to acquaint readers with the tools necessary for effective performance improvement. The tools described in this book are intended to help ensure that performance improvement efforts are

- planned and systematic,
- based on reliable data and accurate analysis, and
- carried out with effective teamwork and communication.

*For more information on the Joint Commission's cycle for improving performance, consult the following publications, available from the Joint Commission: *Framework for Improving Performance: A Guide for Home Care and Hospice Organizations* and *Cycle for Improving Performance: A Pocket Guide.*

Use of these tools, as part of an effective performance-improvement method, will greatly increase the chances that improvement efforts will succeed.

Each of the tools has its own purpose and application. Some tools are creative tools, designed to stimulate new thoughts and solutions for old problems. Some help a team get organized or understand a process. Other tools are more statistical in nature; they are used to collect or analyze data or to display the results of analysis. Each tool can be used effectively on its own, but the greatest benefits are reaped by using the tools together as part of a systematic improvement effort.

This book groups the tools according to their general purposes, placing them in the following categories:

- Tools for planning,
- Tools for teams,
- Tools for data collection,
- Tools for data analysis, and
- Tools for understanding root causes.

Many of the tools can work in more than one category. For example, critical paths, which this book includes as a tool for planning, also can be used for data collection and analysis.

The next sections briefly describe the major tools in each category.

Tools for Planning

Used as a touchstone throughout an organization's efforts to improve its performance, *hoshin planning* is an ongoing, customer-driven effort that helps organizations develop and attain long-range, strategic goals. It is an organizationwide process of developing a vision and taking action that begins when a team develops a picture of an organization functioning in its ideal state. This vision becomes the blueprint for improvement.

Critical paths are products of multidisciplinary planning for optimal care processes. A critical path presents, in an at-a-glance format, the activities performed by various health care professionals to carry out a specific patient care procedure or to treat a specific diagnosis. Critical paths often are developed in conjunction with a new service, but they also may be used to help standardize existing processes. Critical paths can be seen as planning tools, but they are also tools for collecting data and comparing performance; collecting data about variations from the path's specifications can help health care professionals identify potential opportunities for improvement.

Tools for Teams

Brainstorming, affinity diagrams, multivoting, and selection grids are tools used to help a team spur creativity and get started on its improvement task. These tools also are appropriate at any time during the improvement process when a team needs to reorganize and get a fresh perspective on a situation or when a team feels overwhelmed. The tools help draw a team toward agreement in a logical, objective way.

Brainstorming is a creative process used to generate multiple ideas in a minimum amount of time. It involves active participation of all group members and provides a nonjudgmental forum for addressing issues and exploring solutions to problems.

Affinity diagrams are diagrams designed to help teams organize large volumes of ideas or issues into meaningful groups. They bring a recognizable shape to a confusing issue, helping a new team through the initial stages of an improvement effort.

Multivoting is a group technique for narrowing a broad list of ideas down to those that are most important. It frequently is used after a brainstorming session, but can be applied to any list of ideas that needs to be pared down.

Selection grids are tools used to help a team select a single option out of several possibilities. They involve setting important criteria that are used as a basis for reaching a decision acceptable to the group.

Task lists and storyboards are two other useful tools for teams. The *task list* is the most familiar tool of performance improvement. It is no more than a written record of what has been done and what is left to do. It is an easy way to keep the team organized and on track. And sometimes a simple task list can be expanded into an action plan. *Storyboards* are combinations of charts, graphs, and simple text that tell the story of a team's progression through the improvement process. Intended for public display, they are concise summaries of a team's activities. They also are valuable as a kind of "working minutes" for the team along the way.

Tools for Data Collection

Indicators are very specific quantitative measures. Data collected using these measures help show how a process is performing. *Check sheets* are forms that record how often an event or condition (often defined by an indicator) occurs. They are used when a team needs to gather data to measure a process and are a helpful starting point for the more complex charts and diagrams used in performance comparison. The data collected using indicators and check sheets form the basis for other analysis, so it is crucial that these tools are properly used to ensure valid results.

Tools for Analysis

Run charts, control charts, and histograms are all statistical, quantitative tools used to display the performance data of a process so that you can easily analyze the data and compare them to past performance or to your standards or ideals. *Run charts* use the plotting of points on a graph to show levels of performance over time; their purpose is to identify trends and patterns in a process, including movement away from the average.

Control charts are run charts that include statistically determined threshold limits on either side of the average. They are designed to tell what type of variation exists in a process and whether the process is statistically in control. (The Appendix of this book, "Constructing Statistical Control Charts," offers detailed information on these tools.) *Histograms* are important diagnostic tools that display information about the way data are distributed within a range of values. They use a bar chart format to answer questions such as what kind of distribution exists in a group of events.

Tools for Understanding Root Causes

Various statistical and nonstatistical tools can help you uncover the root causes of particular outcomes in a process. Understanding causes is essential if you are to create lasting improvements. Flowcharts and cause-and-effect diagrams are two nonstatistical tools designed to help you understand root causes.

Flowcharts are graphic representations of either the actual or the ideal path that a process follows from start to finish. *Cause-and-effect diagrams*, also called *fishbone diagrams* because of their shape, show the many causal relationships between various actions or events leading to a specific outcome. Both of these tools help you visualize how various components in a process relate to one another and help you draw conclusions and devise solutions to problems.

Pareto charts and scatter diagrams are statistical tools that help you assess performance. *Pareto charts* use a bar graph format to compare the frequency of certain events, problems, or causes. The purpose of a Pareto chart is to show which events or causes are most frequent and have the greatest effect. This information helps you determine what problems to solve and in what order. *Scatter diagrams* are graphs designed to show the correlation between two variables. Staff can use scatter diagrams to gauge the relative strength of their theories and to monitor the effects of their actions.

Who Uses the Tools?

To understand these tools requires an understanding of who carries out performance-improvement activities. Some improvement efforts are carried out by existing work groups, such as a nursing unit or pharmacy department. However, most processes in a hospital involve people in various departments and disciplines. For example, in a hospital, joint replacement surgery requires a cooperative effort of physicians, nurses, discharge planners, rehabilitation specialists, and others.

Therefore, improvement teams often include representatives from various departments, units, disciplines, and levels of the organization.

Using the categories established for the tools, we can examine who might carry out each activity in a hospital and use the relevant tools:

Tools for planning. A planning tool such as hoshin planning would most likely be used by a hospital's senior leaders. Because hoshin planning looks at the big picture of the organization, administrative and clinical leaders must be involved. Of course, input from other staff may be necessary to get a complete picture of the organization for planning purposes.

Creating a critical path requires participation of all staff involved in treating the condition or performing the procedure. When creating critical paths, some organizations also involve clients to ensure that their perspective is considered. Administrators may be involved as well, especially if the critical path involves changes such as the purchase of new equipment.

Tools for teams. Tools for teams, such as brainstorming, affinity diagrams, and multivoting, are appropriate for any group that must come up with ideas, get organized, or make decisions. Whether senior leaders are trying to decide on a strategic direction, whether a team is trying to decide what needs a clinical information system must fulfill, or whether a supervisor and staff are trying to decide how to solve a problem with staff coverage, these tools help keep a group on track and jump-start the group when it is stalled.

Tools for data collection. Tools such as check sheets are used to collect the data on which analysis and improvement actions are based. Staff with statistical expertise can be of great assistance in developing data-collection tools. An improvement team might collect data itself, or the team might use existing sources of data, such as patient satisfaction surveys or outcomes data from medical records.

Tools for analysis. Again, staff with statistical expertise can provide valuable assistance in using quantitative tools such as control charts and scatter diagrams. However, with the knowledge this book provides, most teams will be able to apply these tools with minimal assistance.

Tools for understanding root causes. Tools such as flowcharts, cause-and-effect diagrams, and Pareto charts are designed for use by any group studying a process. With the instruction in this book, any team should be able to use these tools.

Moving Ahead

Having established this context for how and why the tools are used, we can proceed with the tools themselves. The following sections of this book present the tools through

- step-by-step explanations of how each tool is used, and
- examples of how the tools are used.

After the tools are introduced, a case study and an exercise show how the tools may be used as part of a coordinated improvement effort.

Section 2 Tools for Planning

As health care delivery throughout the country continues its rapid transformation, health care professionals are challenged to plan effectively to stay ahead of the changes. The tools in this section can help health care professionals accomplish that goal. These tools can help in overall strategic planning, in planning for performance improvement, and in planning a new service. The tools should *not* be thought of as useful only for a performance improvement "program." Rather, they are useful for all planning activities that leaders and staff undertake.

The two primary planning tools this section focuses on are hoshin planning and critical paths. The section also describes several other tools that health care professionals will find useful for planning.

Hoshin Planning

Hoshin planning helps organizations develop and attain strategic goals by focusing on customer satisfaction and fundamental process improvement.[1] The name comes from the Japanese term *hoshin kanri*, which translates roughly as "policy deployment." Through hoshin planning, an organization

- formulates a plan (the strategic focus, or hoshin);
- transforms the plan into action steps designed to accomplish measurable results (the deployment); and
- audits the plan.

Designed to move an organization toward its long-term goals, hoshin planning is used throughout the process of continuous performance improvement. It is an ongoing effort undertaken by the organization as a whole. Hoshin planning should begin in the earliest phases of the performance improvement process, when an organization's leaders develop a vision of the organization functioning in its ideal state. This vision becomes the blueprint for everything to follow, until it is changed as a result of auditing.

Process

Hoshin planning is an organizationwide process of creating a vision and taking action. It is crucial that management include all members of the organization at some point in hoshin planning. Management also must see that timely progress is made by balancing the work of creating the vision with the processes that will translate vision into action. The following steps outline the hoshin planning process (and incorporate some of the other tools described in this book):

1. **Select stakeholders.** All key leaders of the organization should be selected for participation in the initial planning stages. The group may range in size from 5 to 25, and it should represent the diversity of the organization's constituents. If appropriate, individuals from outside the organization may also be included.
2. **Gather information.** The stakeholders should conduct or actively review current assessments of customer needs and wants, critical environmental issues facing the organization (economic, social, and technological, for example), the organization's position among competitors in the marketplace, and the organization's strengths and weaknesses.
3. **Craft the vision.** Be sure to include each stakeholder in this step. Together, the stakeholders will answer the question, "What would the organization look like ten years from now if it were meeting and exceeding customers' expectations, responding to the environment in which it operates, ideally positioned in the marketplace, and capitalizing on its strengths and weaknesses?" Use brainstorming techniques to record all ideas (see Section 3, pages 37–39).
4. **Develop the elements of the vision.** Create an affinity diagram (see Section 3, pages 40–43, 44) to divide brainstorming ideas into logical groups around common themes. These themes become the vision elements. Expand each element into a full sentence, and join these to form a clear narrative vision.
5. **Create the hoshin (strategic focus).** Drawing a simple interrelationship digraph (see Figure 2-1, page 17) can help accomplish this task. Write each element inside a box or a circle. Consider the elements with respect to each other and draw lines between those that have a relationship. Examine each connection to determine which element influences the other and draw an arrow indicating the direction of influence. The elements with the highest numbers of outgoing arrows (for outputs) are the "key elements," drivers of change, or critical success factors. These elements (choose no more than four) will become the strategic focus, the hoshin, of the organization's work.

Interrelationship Digraph

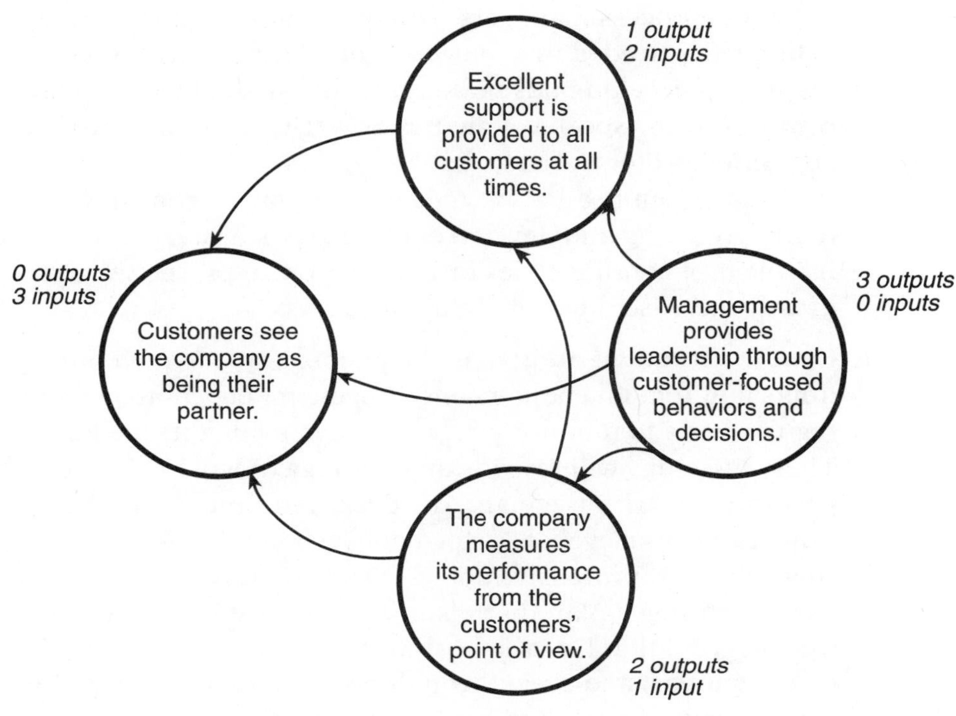

Figure 2-1. *An interrelationship digraph is one tool of hoshin planning. The circles represent elements of the organization's vision. Arrows show the relationship of one element to another. Elements with the most arrows moving away—outputs—are considered the most important. Action plans focus on these elements.*

Source: St Lawrence D, Stinnett B: Powerful planning with simple techniques. *Quality Progress* 27(7):60, 1994. Used with permission.

6. **Operationalize the success factors.** Brainstorm what must be developed or improved in the organization to put the critical success factors into operation. Then build an affinity diagram based on the brainstorming ideas. The headers you create will become the areas for performance breakthrough—that is, the actions necessary to implement the key success factors. To determine which actions will yield the most return, make a selection grid (see Section 3, pages 46–51) that lists breakthrough elements across the top and customer requirements down the side. When the grid is complete, the highest-scoring breakthrough category is the one to pursue first.

7. **Develop breakthrough projects.** At this point, the stakeholders prepare to deploy the hoshin throughout the organization. They define projects with specific, quantifiable targets for improvement based on the breakthrough areas and determine

which managers will take complete ownership of the processes within the projects.

These process managers will form teams to plan the specific action steps needed to achieve the breakthrough targets. The teams will develop budgets, set time lines, and identify who is responsible for specific activities as well as who needs to be kept informed of team actions.

When planning action steps, it is helpful to consider what might go wrong and develop contingency steps. By incorporating the best contingencies into the action steps, the team will greatly increase the probability of success.

8. **Conduct frequent audits.** As the plan is implemented, it is important for stakeholders and process managers to meet on a regular basis to monitor progress and get valuable feedback. These meetings will provide an ongoing comparison of actual performance with the plan. Any deviations, including those in time frame and level of performance, should be placed on a "heat sheet" for intensive analysis and resolution.

   The strategic plan that results can be best illustrated as a tree diagram that lists the hoshin (or strategic focus), breakthrough areas, and breakthrough projects. Figure 2-2 (page 19) shows a generic tree diagram for hoshin planning.

Benefits

Hoshin planning is a customer-driven process that builds important organizational goals from the diverse ideas and values of employees at every level. It is based on the philosophy that people support what they help create. Through collaborative efforts at every stage in the process, the work of the organization becomes aligned with the work goals and aspirations of the individuals responsible for its success. Hoshin planning translates participation into a clear understanding of the organization's vision and into commitment to customer service and performance improvement.

Examples

- A health care organization may want to expand its primary care base in the community (see Figure 2-3, page 20). Hoshin planning will help to organize the critical success factors that must be addressed in order for this to happen, such as gathering information about the community and its need for primary care services, determining appropriate approaches to physician affiliation, recruiting physicians, and determining the appropriate structure for offering primary care services (such as building a single outpatient center or deploying clinics throughout the community).

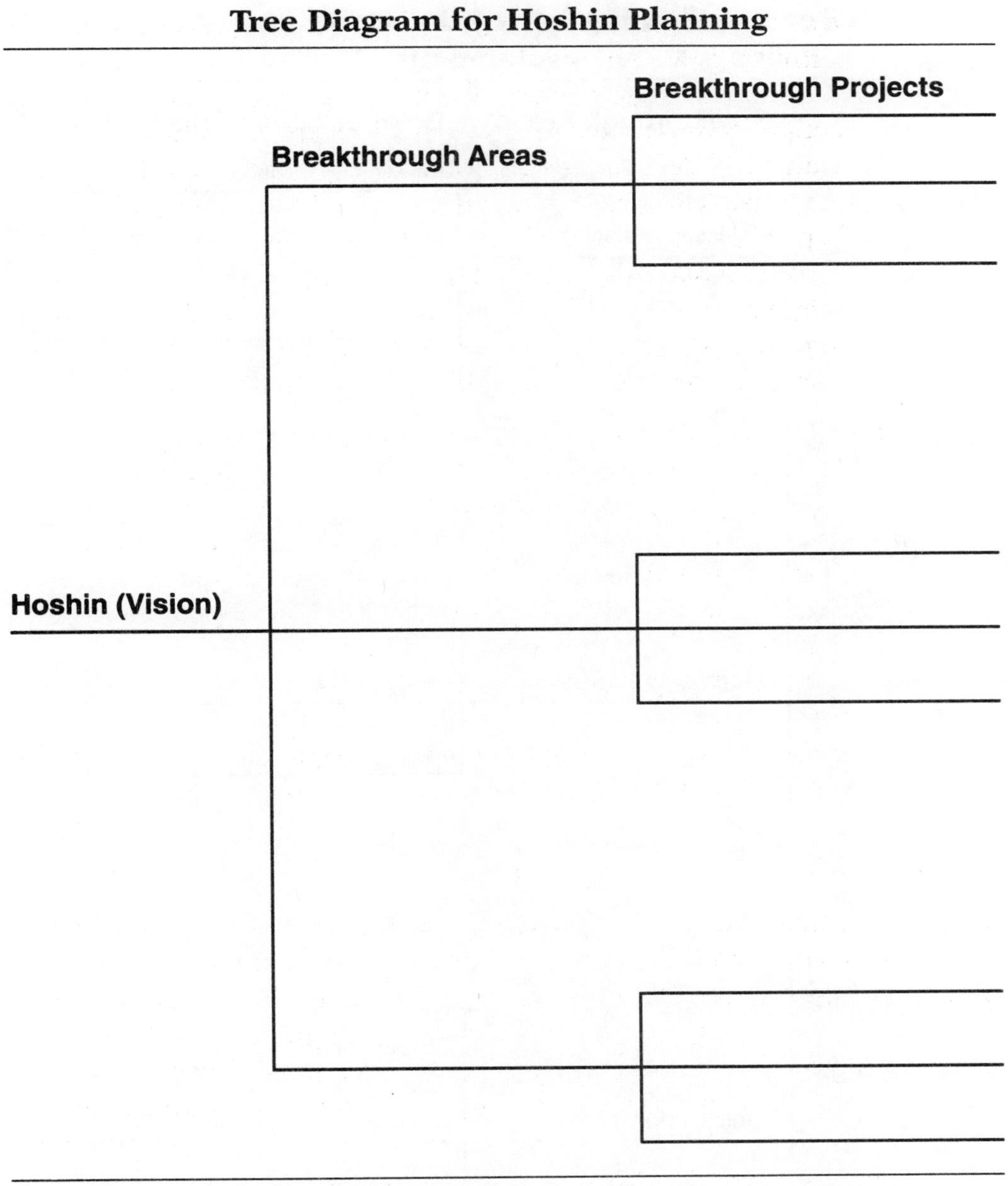

Tree Diagram for Hoshin Planning

Figure 2-2. *This generic tree diagram shows the major phases of hoshin planning and the relationships between those phases. Once planners have established a hoshin—or vision—they determine several general areas in which the hoshin can be implemented. Next, they determine several projects that can be implemented within each of the areas.*

- A medical center consisting of a hospital, a medical school, and affiliated physicians and practice groups used hoshin planning to create a common long-term plan. As the group of stakeholders worked through the hoshin planning process, several possible hoshins were identified. One hoshin was "coordinated governance and planning." The tree diagram in Figure 2-4,

Hoshin Planning in Hospitals:
Primary Care Development

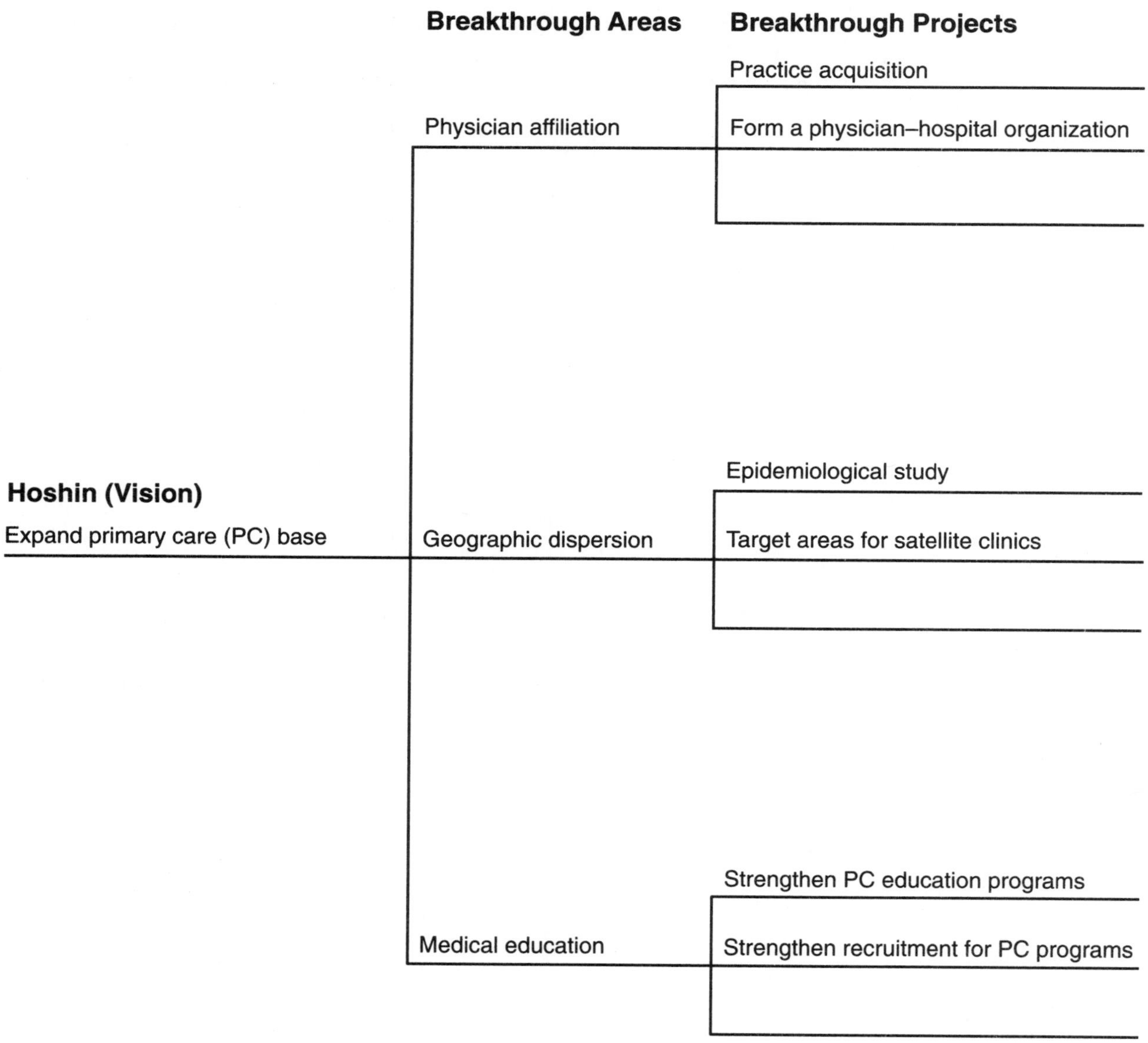

Figure 2-3. *This tree diagram shows an example of the product of hoshin planning: a hoshin that reflects the strategic vision of the organization, several breakthrough areas in which this hoshin can be achieved, and several projects that can be performed to fulfill the goals for each breakthrough area.*

page 21, shows the breakthrough areas and breakthrough projects proposed for this hoshin.

- For an existing service area, such as cardiac care services, hoshin planning may be useful in identifying breakthrough projects to improve the service (which could include projects such

Hoshin Planning in Hospitals: Integrated Systems Development

Hoshin	Breakthrough Areas	Breakthrough Projects
Hoshin Integrated systems	Design ambulatory care system	Ambulatory care facility
		Information system
		Nonuniversity practitioners
	Provide continuum of care	Pre-encounter linkages
		Intra-VAMC* processes
		Discharge plus
	Integrate key business processes	Admitting/scheduling and discharge
		Billing/collecting
		External relations
		Finance/marketing

*VAMC = Vermont Academic Medical Center

Figure 2-4. *This example shows the breakthrough areas and breakthrough projects that must be developed or improved for a medical center to achieve the hoshin of integrating systems.*

Source: Demers DM: Tutorial: Implementing hoshin planning at the Vermont Academic Medical Center. *Quality Management in Health Care* 1(4):69, 1993. Used with permission of David M. Demers, MPH, Medical Center Hospital of Vermont.

as redesigning processes for follow-up care, patient education, or performing specific procedures). Once identified, such projects could be incorporated into the hospital's strategic plan.

- A hospital may identify establishment of a physician–hospital organization as a breakthrough area that will enable the hospital to reach a goal of being a successful bidder for managed care contracts. Hoshin planning can help a planning team identify the key steps necessary to reach the goal. Key steps might include determining the capital investment necessary; studying competing physician–hospital organizations; establishing criteria for physician membership; and establishing the means to divide funds from capitation contracts.

REVIEW OF PROCEDURE

1. Select stakeholders.
2. Gather information.
3. Craft the vision.
4. Develop the elements of the vision.
5. Create the hoshin (strategic focus).
6. Operationalize the success factors.
7. Develop breakthrough projects.
8. Conduct frequent audits.

Critical Paths

Critical paths are comprehensive, flexible frameworks used to guide a single patient-care process. A critical path details the involvement of all groups (physicians, nurses, and other staff) and summarizes their activities, using a day-by-day, at-a-glance format.

Critical paths are frequently developed in conjunction with launching a new service, but they also may be used to redesign an existing process. They should be created when an organization wants to create an "ideal" process for performing a patient care procedure or treating a certain disease. It is important to remember that critical paths do *not* replace an individual caregiver's judgment about a unique situation.

Process

The basic process for designing a critical path is not complicated, but it can be lengthy due to the elaborate and collaborative nature of the task. The following steps are common to most critical path development efforts:

1. **Select the process.** Any new service is a likely candidate. Organizations also are using critical paths to redesign processes that need improved consistency to produce good outcomes cost-effectively. A selection grid might help in choosing an existing process for redesign. The criteria for selection might include volume, risk, problematic nature, cost, and relevance to organization mission. Using a selection grid or other decision-making tool can help ensure agreement that the process chosen is an important one for the organization (see Section 3).

DO'S AND DON'TS OF HOSHIN PLANNING

- **Do** trust the process, include others, show enthusiasm, and be creative.
- **Do** remember that the focus is on the customer, not internal operations.
- **Do** pick a subject or work area in which you are knowledgeable and over which you have a reasonable amount of control.
- **Do** communicate or display the outputs of the planning process frequently and use feedback to improve the plan.
- **Do** integrate these techniques with other methods that have worked for you in the past.
- **Don't** give up until you have tried each technique at least once.
- **Don't** become so caught up with the process and techniques that you forget why you are doing the planning.
- **Don't** try to do too much, so that nothing gets done well.
- **Don't** use the process to prove that your current business plan is right or to convince someone that your ideas are correct.

Source: St Lawrence D, Stinnett B: Powerful planning with simple techniques. *Quality Progress* 27(7):62, 64, 1994.

2. **Define the process.** Participants in the critical path project *must* establish a clear definition of the process being designed or redesigned. The definition should be specific enough to avoid confusion and to avoid creating an overly vague path. However, the definition should not be so narrow that the critical path applies only to a very limited number of cases.
3. **Form a team.** The team should include key users of the process, including physicians, nurses, administrators, and others as appropriate. The team should also get information from patients, even though they are not formally part of the team.
4. **Create the critical path.** Among the most valuable resources for developing the path are the collective knowledge and experience of the team members. The team should discuss the process and use consensus-building tools to create a path that includes key activities for all steps in the process. Team members must support the path and should be flexible and not impose one approach over another. The path should not be limited to clinical activities. Where appropriate, the team should include preadmission and postdischarge steps. The idea is to create a path that is concise and practical for everyday use; one page is a user-friendly length for a critical path. The critical paths shown in Figure 2–5 (pages 24–26)and Figure 2-6 (page 27) can be used as guides for critical-path development.

Critical Path: Uncomplicated Coronary Artery Bypass

	PAT **Date** **Day of Week**	OPS/DOS **Date** **Day of Week**	OR/DOS **Date** **Day of Week**	ICU/DOS **Date** **Day of Week**
Assessments/ Evaluations	Nursing assessment ___ Anesthesia assessment ___ Inter H&P or letter ___ Chart requirements met ___ Consent ___ Admission note ___	Nursing assessment ___ SDA/OPS 0530-0600 ___ Anesthesia assessment ___ Chart requirements met ___	Nursing assessment ___ Chart requirements met ___ Anesthesia assessment ongoing ___	Nursing assessment 7–3 ___ 3–11 ___ 11–7 ___ RT assessment ___ Post-op VS till stable ___ VS protocol ___
Tests	Routine UA ___ EKG ___ Chest x-ray (PA & LAT) ___ Chem 20, CBC, PTT, PT, Plt count ___ Type & cross 4 units/6 units ___ Pregnancy test if ind. ___		ABG's ongoing ___ Heart profile: RBS, LYTES, Ca, Hgb, Hct ___ Co-Oximetry ___	Chest x-ray ___ EKG ___ ABG, CBC, CUN, Cr, PT, PTT, CPK, LDH, Isos ___
Consults	Confirm medical evaluation complete ___			Pulmonary Cardiology Co-manage ___ Cardiac Rehab ___
Treatments		Accurate height/weight ___ Shave/prep ___ Nasal 0_2 ___	Insert PA catheter ___ Insert A-line ___ Apply cardiac monitor ___ Pulse oximetry ___ IABP standby ___ Intubate/ventilator ___ Prep ___ Drape ___ Surgery/bypass ___ Autotransfuser ___ Chest tubes ___ Pacer wires ___ Warming blanket ___ Dressings ___	Bed weight ___ Nurse initiated C&DB ___ Dressing assessed ___ Ventilator ___ RT treatments ___ Autotransfusion ___ Pulse oximetry ___ Hemodynamic monitoring ___ Chest tubes ___ Pacer standby ___ Warming blanket ___ Cardiac monitoring ___
Medications	Confirm availability of autologous blood if ordered ___	Start 2 IV peripheral lines ___ Prophylactic antibiotic pre-op ___	Anesthesia sedation ___ Blood therapy ___	IV ___ IV meds ___ Vasopressors ___ Post-op sedation ___
Activity		ABR ___	ABR ___	ABR ___ Card Rehab passive ROM ___
Diet		NPO ___	NPO ___	NPO ___

Figure 2-5 *This figure shows a two-part critical path form. One part shows a partial critical path for uncomplicated open heart surgery. This critical path documents the patient care activities performed each day for this procedure, dividing those activities into assessments/evaluations, tests, consults, treatments, medications, activity, and diet. The second part of this path is a form for documenting any variance from the critical path procedure.*

Source: Hofmann PA: Critical path method: An important tool for coordinating clinical care. *Jt Comm J Qual Improv* 19(7):239–240, 1993. Used with permission of Mount Clemens General Hospital's (Mount Clemens, MI) cardiac surgeons, cardiologist, nursing staff, and TQM staff.

Critical Path: Uncomplicated Coronary Artery Bypass, *continued*

	PO Day 1 **Date Day of Week**	PO Day 2 **Date Day of Week**	PO Day 3 **Date Day of Week**	PO Day 4 **Date Day of Week**	PO Day 5 **Date Day of Week**
Assessments/ Evaluations	Nursing Assessment 7–3 ___ 3–11 ___ 11–7 ___ RT assessment ___ Nutritional screen ___ VS protocol ___	Nursing Assessment 7–3 ___ 3–11 ___ 11–7 ___ VS protocol ___	Nursing Assessment 7–3 ___ 3–11 ___ 11–7 ___ VS protocol ___	Nursing Assessment 7–3 ___ 3–11 ___ 11–7 ___ VS protocol ___	Nursing Assessment 7–3 ___ 3–11 ___ 11–7 ___ VS protocol ___
Tests	Pre/post extubation ___ ABG's ___ CBC, BUN, Cr, LYTES, CPK, LDH, SGOT, PT, PTT, Plt count ___ EKG ___ Chest x-ray ___	EKG ___ CBC, BUN, Cr, LYTES, CPK, LDH, SGOT, PT, PTT, Plt count ___ Chest x-ray ___	EKG ___ CBC, LYTES ___ Chest x-ray ___		
Consults	Pulmonary rehab ___				
Treatments	Wean/extubate within 12 hours ___ Incentive spirometry ___ Chest physical therapy ___ Weight 06:00 ___ O_2 therapy ___ Dressing changes ___ Cough & deep breathe ___ Cardiac monitoring ___	Pulse oximetry prn ___ Weight 06:00 ___ Incision checks ___ DC dsg prior to transfer ___ Assess for DC chest tubes pacer lines ___ Cardiac monitoring ___ O_2 therapy per RT protocol ___	Weight 06:00 ___ Incision checks ___ Cardiac monitoring ___ O_2 therapy per RT protocol ___	Weight 06:00 ___ Incision checks ___ Cardiac monitoring ___	Weight 06:00 ___ Incision checks ___ Cardiac monitoring ___
Medications	IV ___ IV pain meds ___ Blood therapy ___ Vasopressor ___ Post-op sedation ___	IM to PO pain RX ___ DC IV lines main 1 peripheral IV ___ Routine meds ___	Routine meds ___ Change to heplock ___ PO meds ___	Routine meds ___ DC heplock ___ PO meds ___	Routine meds ___ PO meds ___
Activity	Up in chair ___ Cardiac rehab ___ Pulmonary rehab ___	Amb in room with assistance ___ Cardiac rehab ___ Pulmonary rehab ___	Amb in hall ___ Cardiac rehab ___	Amb in hall ___ Cardiac rehab/TM ___	Amb in hall ___ Shower ___ Cardiac rehab/TM ___
Diet	Cl. liq p extubation ___ Prog to 4 gm Na AHA low cholesterol ___	4 gm Na AHA ___	4 gm Na AHA ___	4 gm Na AHA ___	4 gm Na AHA ___

5. **Make the path a working document.** The time and effort put into creating a critical path will mean nothing if th path is not readily available to those involved in the process on a daily basis. Be sure to distribute the path's final version to all involved staff and make it available in all relevant work areas. Consider providing copies to patients as well. Giving them this important information, along with appropriate explanations, can help increase their understanding about treatment and ease the associated anxieties.

Critical Path: Uncomplicated Coronary Artery Bypass, *continued*

Critical Path: Uncomplicated Open Heart Surgery

Variance Report

Date	Unit	Critical Path Day	Variance/Cause	Action	Signature

Sample Care Map: Uncomplicated Myocardial Infarction

Brighton Medical Center Case Care Map

Case Manager: Profile: Uncomplicated MI (Addressograph)

Patient Problem/ Nursing Diagnosis	DAY 1	DAY 2	DAY 3	DAY 4	DAY 5	DAY 6
Pain R/T ischemia	Patient will verbalize pain or discomfort appropriately to RN	Patient will be pain free	—	—	—	Patient will be pain free at discharge
Activity intolerance R/T ischemia	Patient will be able to tolerate BSC without chest pain Patient can participate in "ADL protocol" without chest pain	Patient can participate in "Physical therapy protocol" without chest pain —	— —	— —	— —	Patient will be discharged at anticipated activity tolerance as evidenced by B/P does not change by 20 torr and HR does not change by ≥ 20 BPM
Knowledge deficit R/T new MI	Patient can state why admitted to hospital Patient will understand the importance of notifying RN of chest pain	Patient will demonstrate a readiness to learn Patient will begin to read MI packet	— Patient will be able to state what an MI and angina are and risk factors and use of sublingual nitrates	— Patient demonstrates understanding of diet by making appropriate choices on menu Patient can verbalize discharge needs	— Patient can verbalize community resources Patient can take own pulse	Patient can verbalize activity restrictions and rationale. Patient can restate discharge instructions. Patient will have completed all MI teaching packet goals.
Anxiety R/T hospitalization	Patient can verbalize fears and concerns related to hospitalization	—	Patient displays appropriate coping skills	—	—	Patient can identify appropriate resources and support systems
Potential for injury R/T bleeding (TPA)	Patient will verbalize understanding of reasons to notify RN of signs of bleeding	—	—	—	—	Patient can state rationale for risk factors of anticoagulant therapy
Potential for alt. in cardiac output R/T myocardial damage 2° MI	B/P, HR, U/O, clear lung sounds and norm. range other hemodynamic parameter with or without intervention will be maintained	—	Maint. B/P — without IV vasoactive Rx	—	—	—
Critical path						
Consults	Notify ER attending and family physician, Social Services, Quality Review, Case Manager	Physical therapy Dietary consultation	Social Services ±home care referral	± Pharmacy consult (coumadin teaching)		
Tests	MCPs q 8° X 3 EKG, routine lab work/coag. CXR, O_2 sat	EKG ± MCP ± 2 D echo ± routine labs ± O_2 sat	± EKG ± schedule Holter monitor	± Holter monitor	± coag. ± routine labs ± schedule stress test	± stress test
Treatments	I and O, weight, IV access, cardiac monitoring, B/P, V/S monitoring	± weight — Same as Day 1	— D/C cardiac monitoring and transfer	IV access — Same as Day 3	IV access —	D/C IV
Meds	± O_2 Ntg ± tPa Ntg ± Regmeds ± Lidocaine ± MS ± Sleeper Heparin ± Tylenol ± Beta Blockers ± Ca channel blockers Anti anxiety agent Stool Softener	Same ± wean Lido ± wean Ntg ± O_2	Same wean Lido wean Ntg	Same Assess anticoag therapy (D/C) heparin and conmder ASA)	— — — —	Discharge prescription with completed discharge form
Diet	Cardiac Diet		—	—	—	—
Activity	Bedrest with BSC ADL protocol	Physical therapy protocol — —	— — —	— — —	—	— — —
Teaching	Orientation to unit and routine Dietary reading material	MI packet progressive dietary teaching	—	Evaluate process and target problems areas ± coumadin teaching info bracelet	—	Discharge instruction review
Discharge Planning		Share care map if appropriate	Update to Social Service from QR transfer to general floor	As per Social Service	Consider outpatient needs	Discharge

Figure 2-6 *This figure shows another example of a critical path format. This format includes patient problem and nursing diagnosis along with the activities carried out to care for the patient.*

Source: Brighton Medical Center, Portland, Maine.

Benefits

Designing and using a critical path results in higher levels of efficiency and improved communication between the various departments and individuals involved in the process. Critical paths also help reduce unnecessary variation in treatment. Successful case histories involving critical paths also show increased skill of staff and other outcomes beneficial to patients, including a reduction in the treatment duration.

Examples

- The first part of Figure 2-5 shows a sample critical path. This path is for performance of uncomplicated coronary artery bypass grafting. Each vertical column indicates one day of treatment. Each horizontal column indicates a type of treatment: assessments and evaluations, tests, consults, treatments, medications, activity, and diet. For each day and each type of treatment—in other words, in each "cell" of the path—specific actions are listed, and there is a space to check whether the action is performed. The second part of Figure 2-5 is a form used to document variations from the path. This information can be used to determine whether the path needs to be modified, whether the circumstances of a specific case require departure from the path, or whether a variation requires further evaluation.
- Figure 2-6 shows a somewhat different approach to critical paths—care maps.[2] This format also divides patient care for an identified diagnosis or procedure by treatment day and types of patient care activity (in this example, consults, tests, treatments, medications, diet, activity, teaching, and discharge planning for treating simple acute myocardial infarction). In addition, the care map lists the expected outcome on each day for a range of patient problems and nursing diagnoses. Thus, the care map becomes a tool for establishing a standard of care and for measuring outcomes at various stages of treatment.

REVIEW OF PROCEDURE

1. Select the process.
2. Define the process.
3. Form a team.
4. Create the critical path.
5. Make the path a working document.

TIPS FOR CREATING A CRITICAL PATH

- Remember to include representatives from all groups involved in the process when creating the critical path. Emphasize that this is a cooperative process designed to address practical issues and improve the process.
- Encourage new perspectives and resist the temptation to cling to established processes. Of course, if something is working well, include it in the critical path.
- Try to reach consensus on all relevant parts of the process, but remain flexible and allow for individual variation.
- Be both comprehensive and concise.
- Try to align the critical path with the organization's strategic goals and other improvement efforts.

Other Planning Tools

Many other planning tools exist and are useful for health care organizations.

Figure 2-7 (page 30) shows the results of a process called *force-field analysis*. This process helps a group identify the forces that support an organization's efforts and those that conflict with those efforts. Force-field analysis can be done for a "big" issue—such as a key aspect of an organization's strategic plan—or for a "smaller" matter, such as a particular work process. Force field analysis involves

- identifying the issue or problem being analyzed;
- identifying the ideal state or situation;
- brainstorming to identify the positive forces—forces helping move toward the ideal state; and
- brainstorming to identify the negative forces—forces working against that ideal state.

These forces can be documented as shown in Figure 2-7. The group can next establish priorities for addressing the negative forces.

Figure 2-8 (page 30) is a Gantt chart, which can help illustrate the time line for a project. Figure 2-9 (pages 31–35) shows a format that organization leaders can use to help answer many of the same questions about an organization's direction and strategic goals that hoshin planning helps answer. Figure 2-10 (page 36) shows three grids that teams can use to plan specific improvement efforts.

Force–Field Analysis:
Forming a Physician–Hospital Organization

Driving Forces →	← Restraining Forces
• Strategic plan to form an integrated delivery system	• Legal and regulatory hurdles
• Growth of managed care and capitation in the area	• Competition of other physician–hospital organizations in the market
• Interest of many physicians in forming such an alliance	• Shortage of primary care physicians
• Community need for greater physician–hospital coordination	• Difficulty establishing means to limit physician panel
• Strong relationships with community physicians	• Difficulty raising sufficient capital

Figure 2-7 *By analyzing the forces that help achieve a goal—in this case, formation of a physician–hospital organization—and the forces that impede achieving the goal, planners can help determine action steps as part of strategic planning.*

Gantt Chart: Implementing an Information System

	Jan	Feb	Mar	Apr	May	Jun	Jul	Aug
	Assess needs							
		Assess current capabilities						
Phase One			Compile request for proposal					
					Assess vendor products			
								Select product

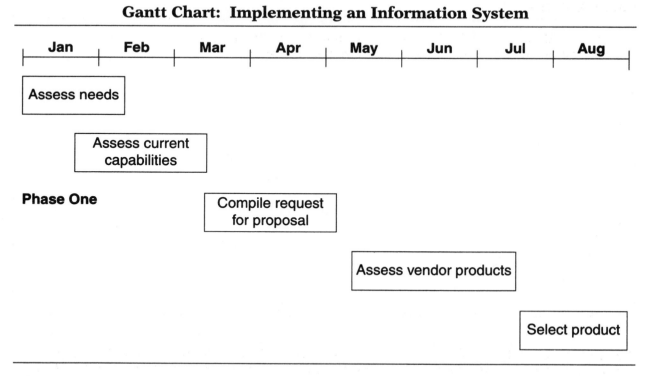

Figure 2-8 *This simple Gantt chart shows a time line for the basic steps an organization might use to select a new information system.*

Organization Analysis Worksheet

1. Products and/or Services:
What are the products and/or services that you produce?

2. Customers:
Who are your customers? Who uses your products and/or services? (This could include internal as well as external customers.)

Figure 2-9 *This worksheet helps an organization's leaders and staff view the organization as a system, begin a system analysis, and decide what processes to improve. The worksheet can be completed for a single department or for an entire organization.*

Source: Developed in a collaborative effort between Executive Learning, Inc, and the Quality Resources Group at Hospital Corporation of America, Nashville, TN. Used with permission.

Organization Analysis Worksheet, *continued*

3. Needs That Products/Services Meet:
What is the underlying social, community, or organizational need that your customers have for your products and/or services?
Do your products and/or services represent the best way to meet these needs?
What might do the job better?

4. Customer Knowledge:
What measures do your customers use when they judge the quality of what you produce?
What prompts customers to use these measures?
Why do your competitors' customers not use your products and/or services?

Organization Analysis Worksheet, *continued*

5. Processes:
What methods or activities do you use to make your products and/or services?
How well are these processes performing?
How do you know?
Are they stable? Are they capable?
Should they be scrapped?
Which processes are core and which support core processes?

6. Inputs:
What comes into your processes and is changed by the process to create the services or products?
How good are the products and/or services you receive?
How do you know?
What could you measure?

Organization Analysis Worksheet, *continued*

7. Suppliers:
What departments, organizations, or people provide the inputs to your processes?
How are they working to improve the products and/or services they provide?
What is your relationship with them?

8. Vision:
Based on your knowledge of your customers and of the underlying social need your organization meets, what is your organization's future goal?

Organization Analysis Worksheet, *continued*

9. Strategic Initiatives:
Based on your vision (and vision of the organization), knowledge of the customer, and information from those knowledgeable about your processes, what are three or four areas/objectives that are strategically important to improve now?

10. Incremental Improvement:
Improvement of which specific processes will create the greatest movement toward the strategic improvements sought by the organization?
How do you know there is a relationship between these processes and the strategic initiatives?
Don't forget to consider processes within your suppliers' organizations as well. What other processes affect the processes you have selected for improvement?

Planning Grids for Improvement

GOAL:					
Strategies	Expected results	Resource requirements	Who's responsible	Target date(s)	Actions

GOAL:				
Strategies	Who	When	Additional results	How to evaluate

GOAL:				
Strategies	Expected results	Additional results	Target date	Action

Figure 2-10 *These three grids can help any group plan and carry out the actions necessary to meet a specific improvement goal. The grids identify various information necessary to oversee improvement activities, including strategies, dates and responsible parties.*

References

1. Demers DM: Tutorial: Implementing hoshin planning at the Vermont Academic Medical Center. *Quality Management in Health Care* 1(4):64–72, 1993.

2. Zander K: Critical pathways. In Melum MM, Sinioris MK (eds): *Total Quality Management: The Health Care Pioneers*. Chicago: American Hospital Publishing, Inc, 1992, p 306.

Section 3 Tools for Teams

Successful performance improvement—like most health care processes—requires effective teamwork. However, teams often struggle because of the unfamiliar tasks and complex problems associated with performance improvement.

The tools in this section are designed to help teams successfully carry out some of their most important activities: generating ideas, organizing ideas, planning tasks, reaching consensus, and documenting accomplishments. In addition, these tools can help a team that is stalled to regain its forward motion.

The tools included are brainstorming, affinity diagrams, multivoting, task lists, selection grids, and storyboards.

Brainstorming

Brainstorming is a creative group process used to generate multiple ideas in a minimum amount of time. It is a starting point for addressing issues and formulating solutions to problems.

Brainstorming can be used any time a team needs multiple ideas or a fresh perspective. It can be used at any stage of the performance improvement process, including planning, determining processes to measure, determining data to collect, interpreting data, and identifying potential improvement actions.

Process

Brainstorming requires clear direction and team effort. It involves the active participation of all group members and facilitation by a group leader. The following steps can be used for effective brainstorming:

1. **Define the subject.** All ideas are valuable in a brainstorming session, as long as they address the subject at hand. The group should be told up front that any idea is welcome, no matter how narrow or broad in scope, how serious or comical in nature. A group brainstorm may be

used to generate lists of topics to assess, process components, topics for data collection, problems, and potential solutions.

2. **Think briefly about the issue.** Allow enough time for team members to gather their thoughts, but not enough time for detailed analysis. Group members should not have time to second-guess their ideas; self-censorship will stifle honesty and creative thought.

3. **Set a time limit.** Agree on a time limit for the expression of ideas. There should be enough time for every member to make a contribution, but not so much time that the team prematurely analyzes ideas. Depending on the size of the group, 10 to 20 minutes should be adequate.

4. **Generate ideas.** This part of brainstorming can follow a structured or unstructured format. No matter the format, *it is crucial that neither the leader nor the other group members comment on any given idea*. Reactions at this stage—whether positive, negative, or indifferent—will be inhibiting and will undermine the process. Be sure to write down every idea as it is stated. If a wordy idea is summarized, make sure to check with the person who offered the idea to ensure that the summary reflects the person's intentions.

   In the structured brainstorming format, group members express ideas by taking turns in a predetermined order; the process continues in rotation until either time runs out or ideas are exhausted. A group member may "pass" his or her turn at any time. This method encourages participation from every member, but may result in a more pressured environment.

   In the unstructured format, group members voice ideas as they come to mind. This method is more relaxed, but unless carefully facilitated, it can lead to domination by more vocal members of the group.

5. **Clarify ideas.** In this final step, the goal is to make sure that all ideas are recorded accurately and are understood by the group. There should be no attempt yet to rank or otherwise judge the ideas. Multivoting, described later in this section, will help with that task.

Benefits

A brainstorming session stimulates creativity and encourages many perspectives on an issue. Because it is a group effort, it also strengthens any team. At the end of a successful brainstorming session, the group will have a varied list that is rich in possibilities.

REVIEW OF PROCEDURE

1. Define the subject.
2. Think briefly about the issue.
3. Set a time limit.
4. Generate ideas.
5. Clarify ideas.

Examples

- Figure 3-1, page 40, shows an example of how an improvement team used brainstorming to generate ideas. In this example, the hospital has determined that its method for reporting potential adverse drug reactions has been unsuccessful and must be redesigned. The team has created a flowchart of the current process and a cause-and-effect diagram of problems with the process. Now the team would like to generate ideas about how the process might be redesigned. As Figure 3-1 shows, the ideas vary widely, and some seem more viable than others. That is intended; brainstorming is for generating ideas, not sorting or judging them.

- A team charged with developing a new hospitalwide information system could use brainstorming at several key points in the process, including identifying current information management needs in each department, identifying current cross-departmental information management needs, and identifying ideal information management capabilities. Such ideas, once adequately reviewed and organized, could help in developing specifications for a request-for-proposal submitted to information system vendors.

TIPS FOR SUCCESSFUL BRAINSTORMING

- Create a nonthreatening environment for expression of ideas.
- Never criticize ideas.
- Write down all ideas so that the group can view them.
- Keep the process short; enforce a time limit of 10 to 20 minutes.

Improvement Team Minutes (Excerpt)

Team: Adverse drug reaction (ADR) reporting

Date: March 2, 1996

Attendance: All present

Team leader suggested the group brainstorm to come up with ideas about elements to include in a redesigned process. The following ideas were generated:

- Broaden definition of "adverse drug reaction"
- Narrow definition of "adverse drug reaction"
- Let pharmacists review each potential reaction
- Provide regular in-service education to nurses about the importance of reporting ADRs
- Implement pager system for reporting ADRs
- Make ADR reporting anonymous
- Identify on-call physician to review each potential ADR
- Create simplified form for ADR reporting
- Review literature for other ADR reporting processes
- Hire more staff

Team proceeded to use multivoting to help reach consensus about which ideas might be the most viable. . . .

Figure 3-1 *This excerpt from an improvement team meeting's minutes shows how brainstorming can be used to generate a wide range of ideas, without judging those ideas.*

Affinity Diagrams

Affinity diagrams are designed to help teams organize large volumes of ideas or issues into meaningful groups. They provide structure and organization where disorder exists, and they can give new perspective to old problems.

Affinity diagrams are particularly useful at the start of a project because they help teams identify and focus on major issues; they are also used in solution planning. They are an effective way to combat feelings of panic when a situation or task appears overwhelming. Affinity diagrams also can be used to transform verbatim comments from a survey or ideas from brainstorming into useful groups.

Process

Use the following steps to create an affinity diagram and achieve a clearer understanding of the issues a team faces:

1. **Choose a team.** The team should consist of four to six people who have varied perspectives on the issue to be addressed. Keeping the group small helps the process.

2. **Define the issue.** Define the issue at hand in the broadest and most neutral manner possible to ensure that results are not skewed—for example, "issues related to joining a community health information network (CHIN)" or "methods to educate patients prior to elective surgery."

3. **Brainstorm the issue.** Record each idea about the issue on an index card or adhesive note. Criticism of ideas is not appropriate at this stage, although asking for clarification is acceptable. State ideas in an understandable manner, whether in complete sentences or in phrases—for example, an understandable statement for the CHIN example might be "Potential violations of patient confidentiality."

4. **Randomly display cards or notes.** After all ideas are recorded, place the cards or notes on a wall or table so everyone can see them.

5. **Sort in silence.** Without talking, members of the team should sort the cards into groups of related topics. This should be done quickly, without time for contemplation. Team members may rearrange a card but not discuss it. Sorting should continue in this manner until all cards are sorted and consensus is reached—which occurs when team members agree to leave all cards where they are.

6. **Create header cards.** Now discuss each grouping and create a title or header for it. Titles must be concise and make sense even out of context. The team may break large groupings into subgroups with subtitles, but should be careful not to slow progress with too much definition. Appropriate subtitles under the CHIN topic might be "cost" and "technology."

7. **Draw the diagram.** Using the identified groups as a reference, draw an affinity diagram such as the one shown in Figure 3-2

(below). Review the diagram with team members and with all non-team members who may be involved when the issue is studied further.

Benefits

Creating an affinity diagram brings a recognizable shape to a seemingly shapeless issue and can help a new team through the initial panic stage when a task seems too large or complex. An affinity diagram also can help a group narrow its focus or divide tasks in a sensible fashion.

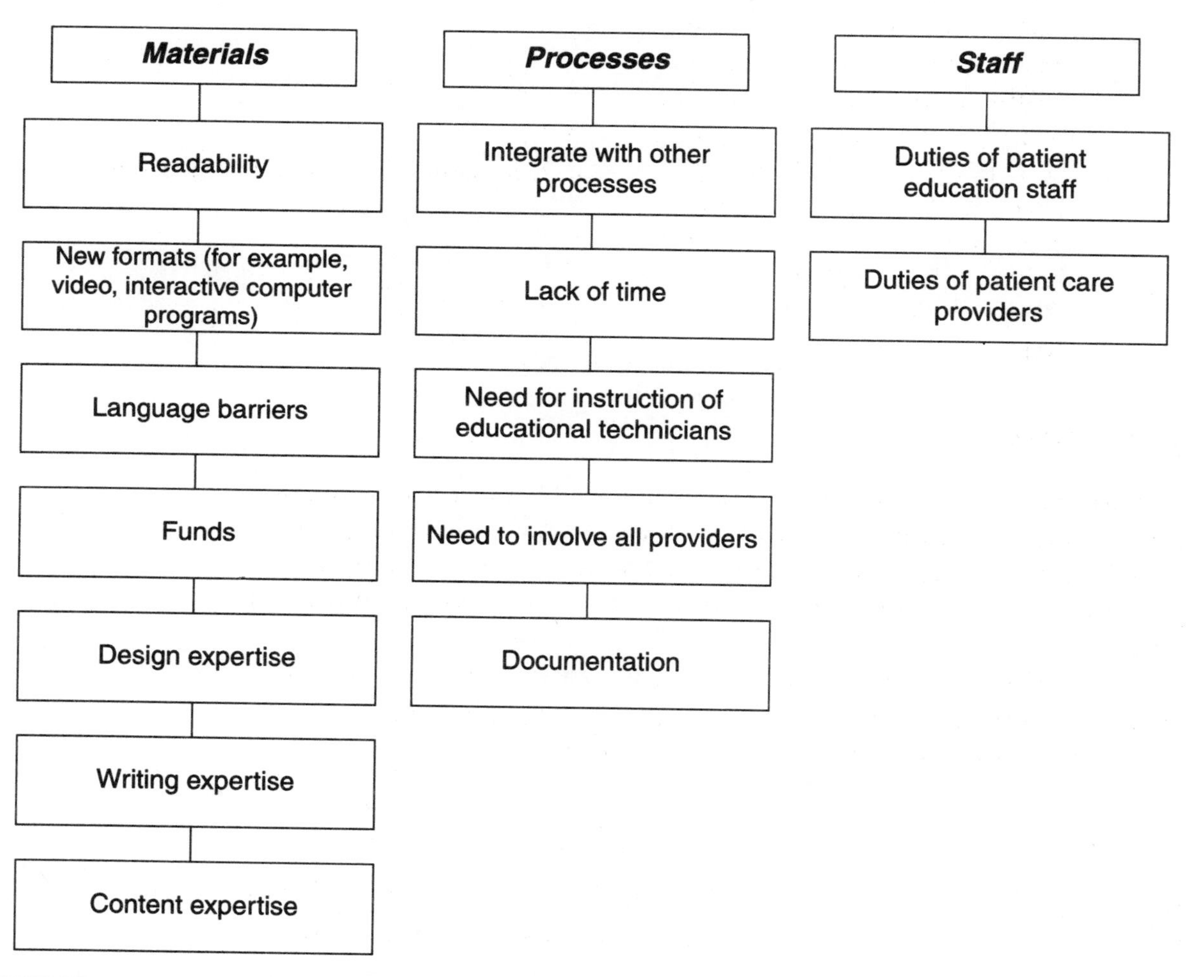

Figure 3-2 *This affinity diagram shows how a team might sort a variety of ideas related to improving patient education.*

Examples

- The affinity diagram in Figure 3-2 shows how a team might sort various ideas pertaining to improving patient education. This affinity diagram might be used to help the team organize potential improvement and challenges associated with redesigning the existing patient education process. This diagram, with its clear categories of materials, processes, and staff, could help the team to better grasp a complex process.

- The example in Figure 3-3 (page 44) shows a unique combination of affinity diagram and flowchart. (Flowcharts are described in Section 6, pages 99–103.) This diagram illustrates various steps in the aminoglycoside dosing and monitoring process according to four categories: prescribing, dispensing, administering, and monitoring. Although this diagram requires a more sophisticated sorting than a traditional affinity diagram, it can help a team understand not just the categories of various ideas or activities, but their sequence as well.

REVIEW OF PROCEDURE

1. Choose a team.
2. Define the issue.
3. Brainstorm the issue.
4. Randomly display cards or notes.
5. Sort in silence.
6. Create header cards.
7. Draw the diagram.

Multivoting

Multivoting is a technique for narrowing a broad list of ideas down to those that are most important. Multivoting is not designed to leave the team with a single idea; using this technique, members of a team work together to determine which are the few critical ideas worthy of immediate attention.

Multivoting is another tool that can be used at all phases of performance improvement. It frequently is used after a brainstorming session, but you can apply it to any list of ideas that needs to be pared down.

Process

Multivoting requires a predetermined list of ideas and a designated team member to guide the group through the process, using the following steps:

1. **Consider whether any items are the same or similar.** Almost any list will have some overlap; this step will simply identify those cases.

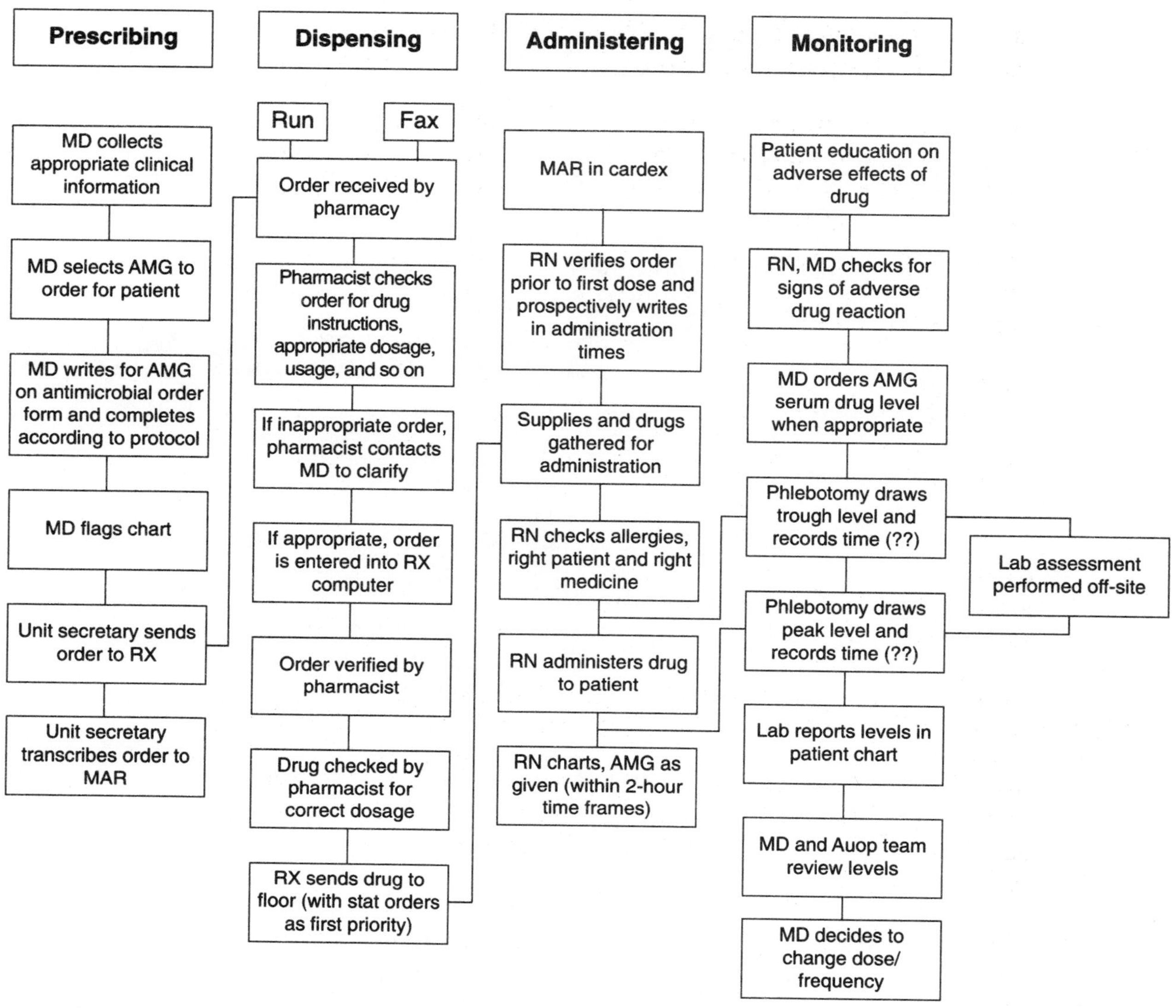

Figure 3-3 *When documenting the current process for dosing and monitoring aminoglycosides, this team found it could establish an affinity diagram—which divided the process into the categories prescribing, dispensing, administering, and monitoring—that also functions as a flowchart, showing the sequence of steps in the process.*

Source: Saint Vincent Healthcare System, Worcester, MA. Used with permission.

2. **Ask the team whether similar items may be grouped together.** The key is *asking*. Faith in the process will be damaged if members feel that their ideas are being altered without permission.

3. **If the group agrees, combine duplicate or similar items.** Each group member—especially those who gave the ideas in question—should agree on the new wording.

4. **Number items on the new list.** Numbering helps the team readily refer to specific items on the list.

5. **Determine the number of points that will be assigned to the list by each group member.** Each member uses points to vote on different items on the list. A typical number of points would be between 5 and 10. One easy way to determine the number of points each member will distribute is to divide the total number of items on the list by 4. For example, if there are 20 items, each member would have 5 points to distribute.

6. **Allow time for group members to independently assign points.** Members are allowed to distribute points any way they want. However, a team may want to adopt the guideline that not all votes can be cast for a single item, which can cause a stalemate.

7. **Indicate each member's point allocation on the list.** Gather each member's votes, and mark those votes on the list next to each item.

8. **Tally the votes.** Write the total for each item so that the team can see the results.

9. **Note items with the greatest number of points.** Often, one or more ideas will be the obvious favorites; sometimes a clear second and third tier will emerge. Occasionally, the votes will be evenly distributed, with no clear preferences.

10. **Choose the final group or multivote again.** If a group of items is clearly the team's preference, this group is considered the final list. If points are too evenly distributed, the team may multivote again, leaving out the two or three lowest items or reducing the number of points each member can assign.

Benefits

Multivoting moves the team in the direction of consensus by means of a diplomatic, nonthreatening selection process. It is a technique that allows several or all of the members to have one of their ideas chosen for further attention. Multivoting effectively limits choices, yet leaves the group a range of choice among the best ideas the team has to offer.

Examples

- Figure 3-4 (page 47) uses the ideas generated in the brainstorming example regarding improving adverse drug reaction reporting (see Figure 3-1). This figure shows how multivoting can be used to move the group toward consensus about which ideas to focus on.
- Figure 3-5 (page 47) shows how a multidisciplinary team might use multivoting to reach consensus on which improvement opportunities related to general surgery might be addressed by an improvement team.

REVIEW OF PROCEDURE

1. Consider whether any items are the same or similar.
2. Ask the team whether similar items may be grouped together.
3. If the group agrees, combine duplicate or similar items.
4. Number items on the new list.
5. Determine the number of points that will be assigned to the list by each group member.
6. Allow time for group members to independently assign points.
7. Indicate each member's point allocation on the list.
8. Tally the votes.
9. Note items with the greatest number of points.
10. Choose the final group or multivote again.

Selection Grids

Also known as *prioritization matrices*, selection grids help a team select a single option out of several possibilities. They involve setting important criteria that are used as a basis for reaching a decision acceptable to the group.

Selection grids are best used when a team faces a list of problems to be solved at the beginning of the performance improvement process or toward the end of the process, when a single solution must be selected from several possible solutions.

Process

The following steps are used to create a selection/prioritization grid:

1. **Start with a list of options.** The list should be fairly limited at the outset. More than eight options will complicate the grid and the selection process.

Multivoting: Selecting Possible Actions to Improve Adverse Drug Reaction (ADR) Reporting

Improvement Action	*# of Votes*
Broaden ADR definition	1
Narrow ADR definition	7
Have pharmacists review each potential ADR	7
In-service education	5
Pager system	2
Identify on-call physician to review potential ADRs	1
Simplify ADR reporting form	6
Review literature for other ADR processes	6

Figure 3-4 *This figure shows how ideas generated by brainstorming might next be subjected to multivoting to identify the most promising candidates to pursue.*

Multivoting: Selecting Improvement Priorities for General Surgery

Improvement Area	*# of Votes*
Blood use	2
Discharge planning	7
Anesthesia use	3
Admissions	3
Patient education	7
Coordination of care	8

Figure 3-5 *This figure shows the results of multivoting used to narrow down several broad areas for possible improvement involved in general surgery.*

2. **Choose criteria and a scoring system.** No more than four or five criteria, stated in either positive or negative terms, should be used; they may be acquired by brainstorming and multivoting. Once the criteria are defined, a scoring system must be established. The team may choose a simple yes/no system to indicate whether a criterion is met, or adopt this four-point scoring system: 1 = very important, 2 = important, 3 = slightly important, 4 = not important. If the team wants to assign weights to the various criteria, this should be done prior to any judging.
3. **Draw the grid.** List criteria across the top of a page and options down the left side; then draw a grid so that there is a box (cell) to represent each possible combination of criteria and options. A final column should be included at the right edge to show the total score for each option. (See Figure 3-6, page 49, and Figure 3-7, page 50, for selection grid examples.)
4. **Judge each option against the criteria and write in the scores.** This step should be completed by the team as a whole, facilitated by the leader, and displayed for all to see.
5. **Use the completed grid to evaluate findings.** Ask the following questions: Does one or more option clearly meet all the criteria? Have any options been clearly eliminated? If an option meets most but not all of the criteria, is it still worth considering?
6. **Determine whether new criteria, or adjustments to existing criteria, are necessary.** If all or most of the options meet most or all of the criteria, some change in the criteria may be necessary.
7. **Select the best option.** Using the scoring system, select the option or options that best fulfill the criteria.

Benefits

Selection grids draw a team toward consensus in a logical, objective way that reassures team members of the validity of the decision-making process. A selection grid can also be used to establish priorities among various options.

Examples

- Figure 3-6 shows a selection grid for establishing improvement priorities. In this case, the criteria for establishing priorities are quality of care, patient satisfaction, staff satisfaction, and cost savings. Other possible criteria include cost to implement change, external customer satisfaction, relationship to

Selection Grid: Improvement Priorities

Decision factor / Process	Quality of care	Managed care contracting	Patient satisfaction	Staff satisfaction	Cost control	Total
Computer-based patient record						
Emergency medical delivery						
Admission process						
Emergency department patient flow						
Pneumonia care						
CABG performance						

Key to Scoring:

X = strong effect	X = 3
0 = some effect	0 = 2
– = weak effect	– = 1
= no effect	= 0

Figure 3-6 *This figure shows a selection grid that could be used to set priorities for improvement among identified opportunities. Scores are assigned to indicate how heavily the decision factor applies to each opportunity. Once the scores are totaled, they should indicate the priority of each opportunity as it relates to the listed decision factors.*

organization's strategic plan or mission, and risk for patients or the organization. Sometimes not all criteria are weighted equally. For example, risk to patients may carry greater weight than employee satisfaction.

- Figure 3-7 shows a somewhat different approach to a selection grid. In this example, no voting is involved. The grid simply displays which of the elements along the vertical axis—in this case, improvement tools—are relevant to the elements along the horizontal axis—in this case, improvement tasks.

Selection Grid: Improvement Tools

Tool Selection Grid

Tool	Phase of Problem Solving Activity			
	Problem Identification	*Data Analysis*	*Solution Planning*	*Evaluating Indicators*
Brainstorming	X	X	X	X
Cause-and-Effect Diagram (Fishbone Diagram)	X	X		
Check Sheet		X		
Control Chart	X	X		X
Flowchart	X	X	X	
Affinity Diagram	X		X	
Histograms		X		X
Multivoting	X	X	X	X
Pareto Analysis	X	X		X
Run Chart	X	X		X
Scatter Diagram		X		X
Selection Grid (Prioritization Matrix)	X		X	
Task List	X		X	

Figure 3-7 *This selection grid is a simplified version of the grid shown in Figure 3-6. In this example, the grid is used to indicate which improvement tools are used in various stages of performance improvement.*

REVIEW OF PROCEDURE

1. Start with a list of options.
2. Choose criteria and a scoring system.
3. Draw the grid.
4. Judge each option, against the criteria and write in the scores.
5. Use the completed grid to evaluate the findings.
6. Determine whether new criteria, or adjustments to existing criteria, are necessary.
7. Select the best option.

Task Lists

Task lists are the most familiar performance improvement tools. They are simply lists of things to be done or to be obtained. Task lists are used to inventory information and keep track of tasks to be done so that nothing is overlooked. Creating a task list is appropriate during any stage in the improvement process.

Process

Even if more informal lists are used by team members every day, the following procedure may enhance the effectiveness of this tool:

1. **Brainstorm what needs to be done or collected.**
2. **Write all items down.** It is helpful if everyone on the team can view the list.
3. **Decide details about the tasks.** Decisions include who will do each task, who else needs to be involved, when the tasks should be accomplished, and any other information necessary for accomplishing the tasks.
4. **Organize information in chart form.** The form should list responsible parties and due dates, and it should include a space to check when each task is complete.
5. **Check off each item on the chart as it is completed.**

Benefits

Task lists are an easy way to keep the team organized and on track, and they are a written record of what has been done and what is left to do. Sometimes a simple task list can be expanded into an action plan.

Examples

- Figure 3-8 (below) gives an example of how a task list can be expanded into an action plan. In this case, a team has to collect certain data and information for an improvement project related to implementing standing orders for treating congestive heart failure.

Storyboards

Storyboards are combinations of charts, graphs, and simple text that, presented as a whole, tell the story of a team's progression through the improvement process.[1,2] Intended for public display, storyboards are concise summaries of your team's activities. They are used to communicate the team's efforts to colleagues and supervisors so that they can give feedback and recognition, understand the improvement process, and learn from the team's experience.

Storyboards are valuable not only as finished products that show a picture of the team's completed work but also as a kind of "working minutes" for the team along the way. They are most helpful when created as part of the very process that they describe. Teams should begin storyboarding at their first meeting and continue building their display as they advance through the improvement process.

Task List/Action Plan: Congestive Heart Failure Standing Order Team

Task	*Person (s) Responsible*	*Due Date*
Collect information on current practices	JL, TT	April 3
Collect information on state of the art	MB, WK	April 3
Identify data elements for outcomes measurement	JL, FM	April 20
Assess staff reaction to current practices	BN, VL	April 20

Figure 3-8 *This figure illustrates the ease with which a list of tasks can be transformed into an action plan. Such plans are helpful at all stages of the improvement process to make sure responsibility and deadlines are assigned for key activities, avoiding delay that occurs when a task "falls through the cracks."*

Process

Storyboards generally follow the style of a flowchart, with a sequence of boxes containing information about each step in the process. Storyboard components can include names of team members, descriptions of the project and why it was selected, situation analysis, data collection/analysis, team actions, and evaluation of results. Most teams find it useful to structure the storyboard according to the steps of the improvement method they use. Figure 3-9 (below) shows a storyboard format that follows the FOCUS-PDCA© process. Figures 3-10 through 3-12 (pages 54–59) show completed storyboards.

Basic Storyboard Format

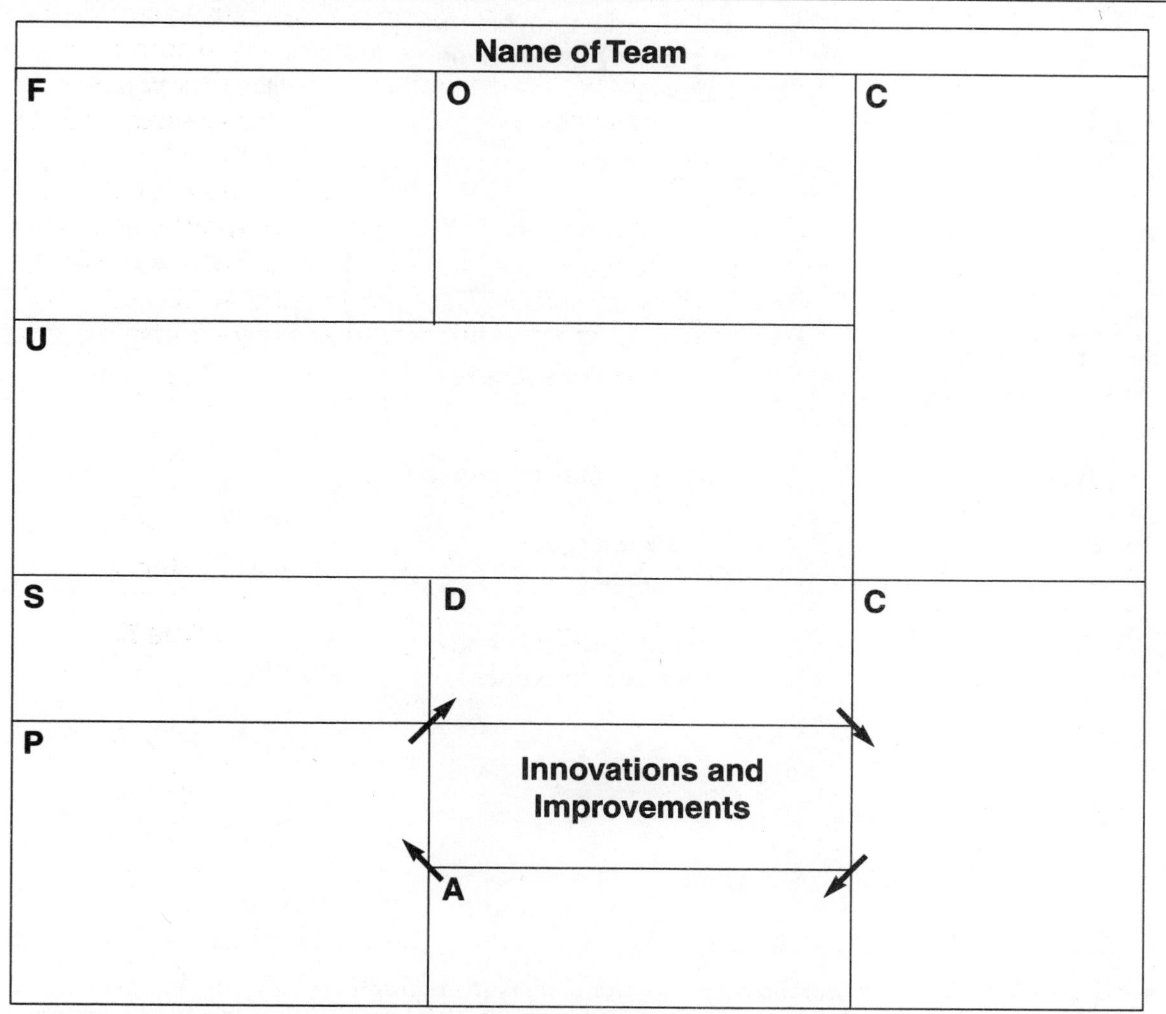

Figure 3-9 *This storyboard follows the FOCUS-PDCA© improvement process. Team activities for each step are documented using written descriptions, charts, and graphs, as appropriate.*

Source: West Paces Medical Center, Atlanta. Used with permission.

Storyboard: Total Knee Replacement

Departments: multidisciplinary

Project definition: develop total knee replacement pathway

Changes and enhancements to total knee replacement

- Developed total knee replacement pathway involving physicians, nursing staff, registration, lab, OR, rehab, and other services.
- Will make improvements in pathway as evaluations indicate.

Monitoring information

- Monitored length of stay and total charges prior to instituting pathway.
- Will monitor length of stay and total charges for period after the pathway is in effect.
- Will evaluate patient outcomes after six months.

Pathway implemented February 1995

Important functions and dimensions of performance

- Availability
- Effectiveness
- Appropriateness

Measure of success

- Length of stay decreased
- Patient charges decreased
- Patient outcomes and satisfaction increase

The team

-
-
-
-
-
-
-
-

Figure 3-10 *This is a simple storyboard format for displaying an improvement team's key activities. This storyboard pertains to a total knee replacement improvement project. The storyboard's components are departments, changes and enhancements, monitoring information, important function and dimension of performance, measure of success, and team members.*

Source: Kathy Moody, QI Data Specialist. Watertown Memorial Hospital, Watertown, WI. Used with permission.

Storyboard: C-Section Response Time

Departments: Newbirth Center (NBC), Surgery, Medical Staff

Project definition: Improve response time for emergency C-sections to comply with American College of Obstetrics and Gynecology guidelines

Changes and enhancements to emergency C-sections

- Monitoring showed excessive time elapsed from decision to do emergency C-section.
- Developed "STAT nurse to NBC" page system.
- Trained NBC staff to set up C-section pack so OR is ready when staff arrives.

Monitoring information

- Monitoring eight months response times prior to improvement showed response times greater than 30 minutes.
- New process is being monitored and adjustments made as indicated by data.

Improvements implemented February 1995

Important functions and dimensions of performance

- Timeliness
- Availability
- Efficacy
- Safety
- Treatment, performance improvement

Measure of success

- Time from decision to perform emergency C-section to time of delivery of infant dropped to less than 30 minutes in compliance with ACOG guidelines.

The team

-
-
-
-
-
-
-
-

Watertown Memorial Hospital, Watertown, WI

Figure 3-11 *This is another example of the format shown in Figure 3-10. In this case, the storyboard shows activities related to improving response time for emergency Cesarian-Sections (C-sections).*

Source: Kathy Moody, QI Data Specialist. Watertown Memorial Hospital, Watertown, WI. Used with permission.

Storyboard: Laboratory Cerebrospinal Fluid (CSF) Processing

Facility: Lutheran General Hospital HealthSystem	Contact:	
Project: Laboratory CSF Processing	Phone:	

Find a process to improve

Origin

Insufficient quantity of specimen

- Turnaround time (TAT) was too long
- No single location for specimen storage
- Orders not clarified

Boundaries

- Begins: The point at which the CSF specimen is received in the specimen-receiving area of the laboratory
- Ends: The point at which the laboratory reports the results

Aim

- Decrease number of CSF specimens received with insufficient quantity
- Decrease TAT of CSF processing
- Decrease time to locate sufficient volume of specimen to perform ordered tests

Organize an effort to work on improvement

- Team Leader:
  - Takashi Okuno, MD, Clinical Laboratories
- Facilitator
- Team members:
  - Bacteriology
  - Biochemistry
  - Cytology
  - Hematology
  - Immunovirology
  - Laboratory Administration
  - Laboratory Quality Assurance
  - Laboratory Information Specimen Acquisition

Figure 3-12 *This storyboard—more elaborate than the examples in Figures 3-10 and 3-11—follows the FOCUS improvement process and shows team members, flowcharts, key quality characteristics, and results. Such a flowchart can be a great asset for demonstrating to formal and informal groups the progress and accomplishments of an improvement effort.*

Source: Lutheran General Hospital, Park Ridge, IL. Used with permission.

Storyboard: Laboratory Cerebrospinal Fluid (CSF) Processing, *continued*

Clarify current knowledge of the process

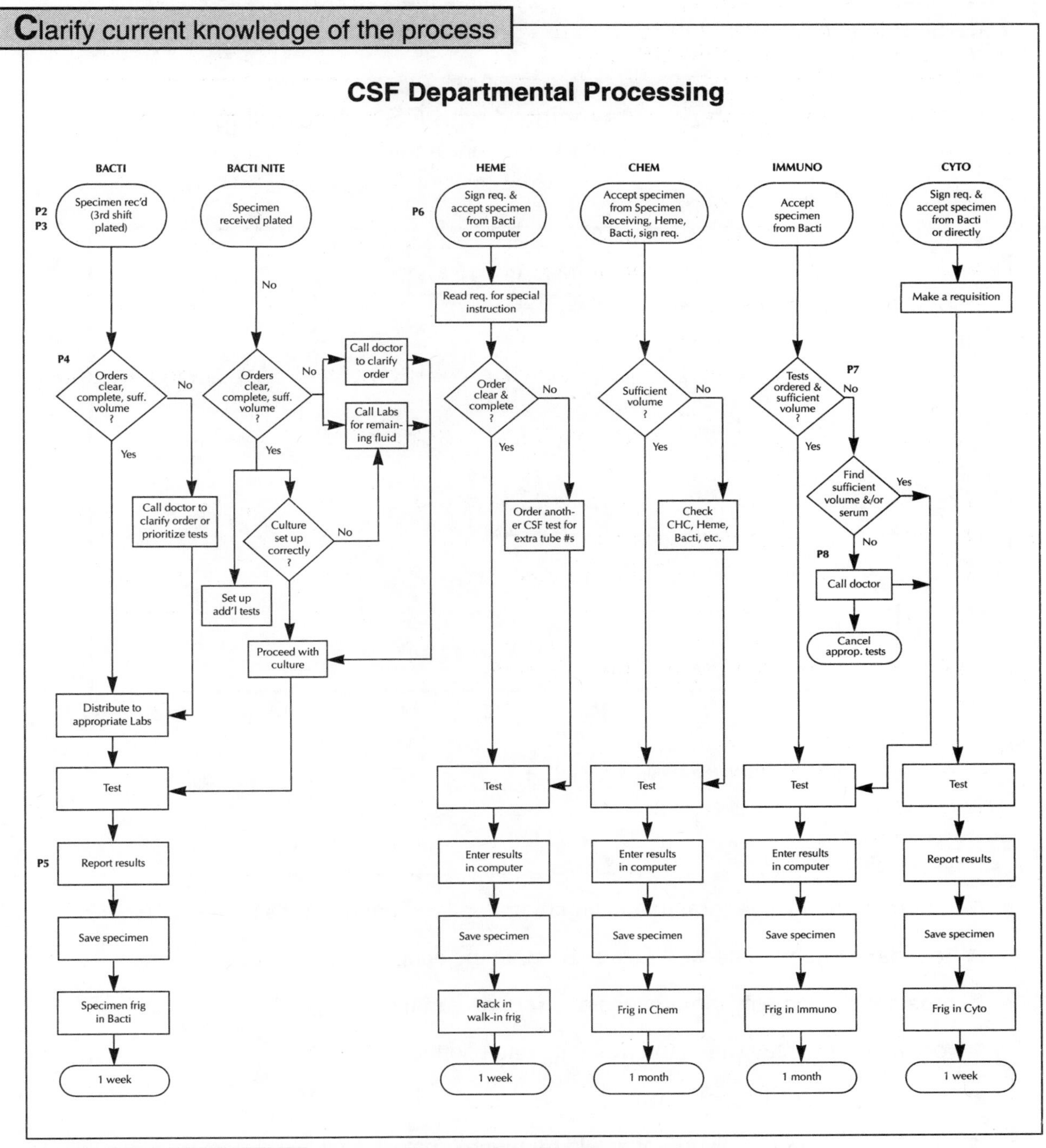

Key quality characteristics:	Accurate and timely results of CSF specimens

- Percent of CSF specimens received with any of the following problems:
  - Insufficient specimen
  - Mislabeled specimen
  - Lost specimen
  - Unclear specimen
  - Other
- Number of telephone calls that Bacteriology must make because of problems with CSF specimens
- Departmental satisfaction with CSF process

Storyboard: Laboratory Cerebrospinal Fluid (CSF) Processing, *continued*

Understand process variation and capability

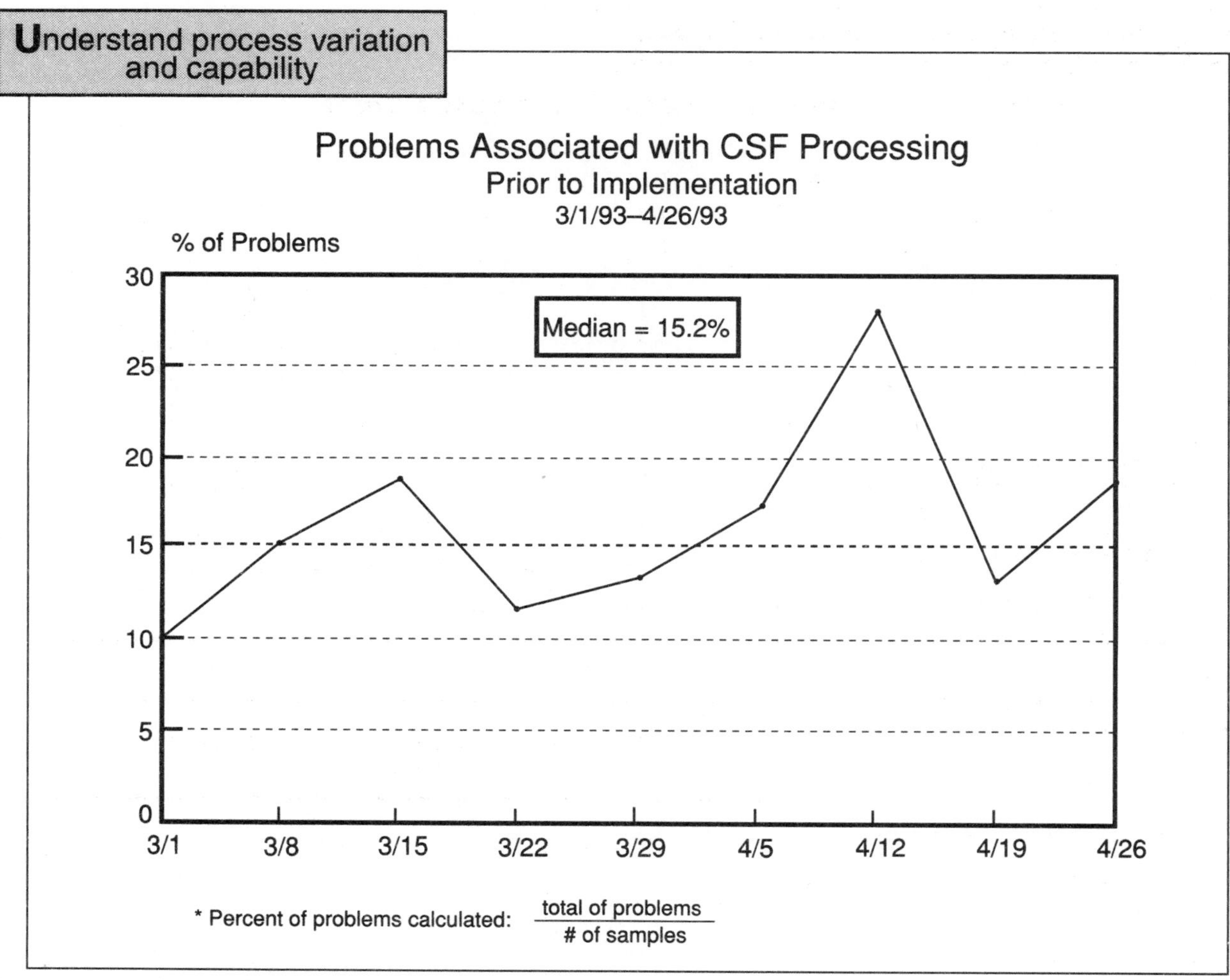

Lessons learned

- Important for each laboratory section to understand each other's process
- Boundaries need to be workable and within the scope of authority of the group
- Imperative to simplify the process and reduce variation
- Very difficult to stay within the meeting time allotted
- The CQI process is a lot of work
- Intense staff level involvement would be much more difficult
- Meeting minutes, flowcharts, and data collection required a lot of preparation time
- Data collection continues after implementation of the process improvement

Storyboard: Laboratory Cerebrospinal Fluid (CSF) Processing, *continued*

Select a strategy for continued improvement

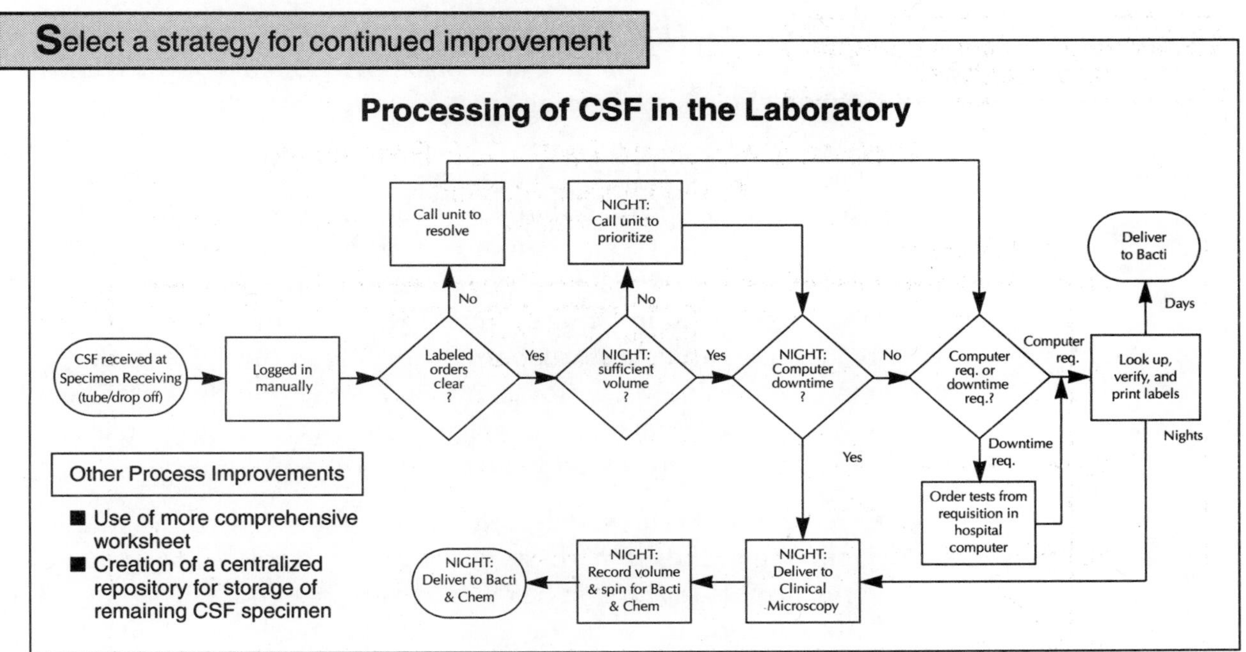

Other Process Improvements

- Use of more comprehensive worksheet
- Creation of a centralized repository for storage of remaining CSF specimen

Major accomplishments

- Modified the CSF HIS computer screen
- Educated medical staff about testing requirements
- Communicated time Bacteriology ends processing at night
- Communicated the cut-off time between third and first shift
- Modified the CSF worksheet to obtain all the necessary signatures and centralize information for the data-collection process
- Created a centrally located CSF retention location
- Modified reporting on the computer-generated patient summary. Now all CSF results are consolidated into one location.

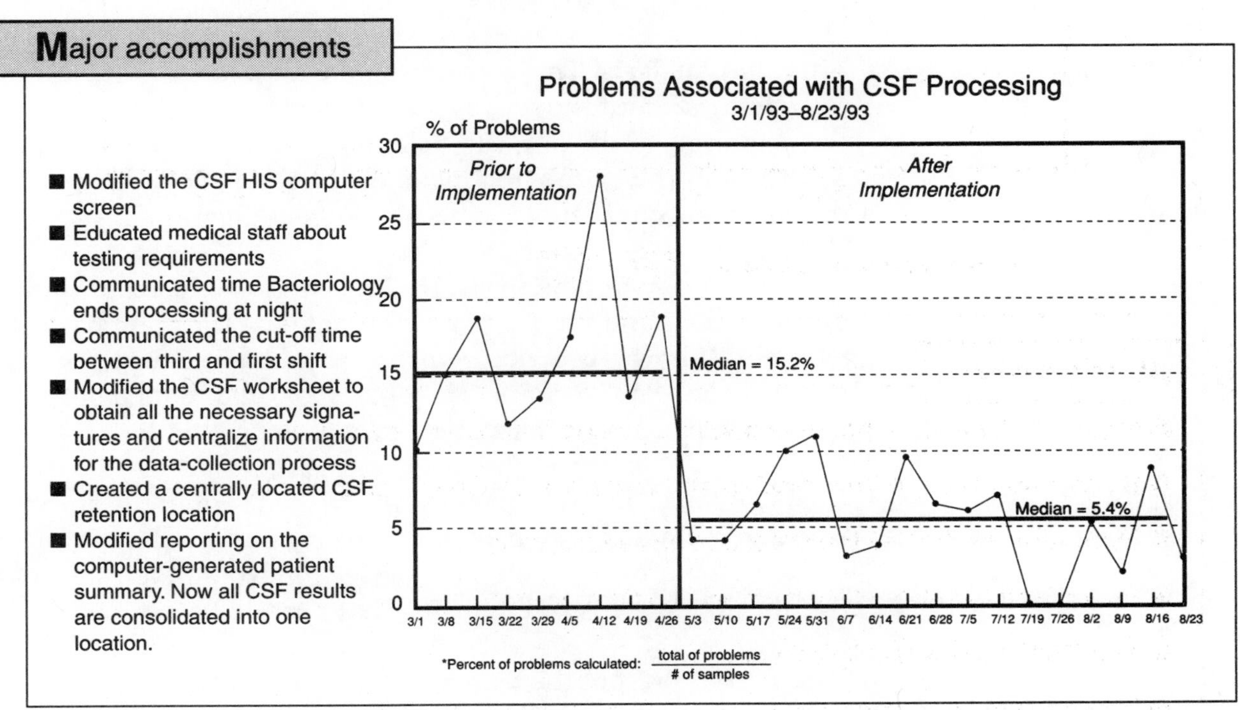

Ultimately, the storyboard should be one that works well for your team, so feel free to choose other components and design a unique layout.

The team should select a size and layout that team members feel comfortable with and that includes the basic components of the team's activities. When choosing materials, make sure the storyboard will be both durable and easy to transport.

The team should feel free to add boxes as needed. The storyboard should be a working document that can be updated after each meeting. One way to update a storyboard is to use adhesive notes. Once a particular stage of a project is completed, the information on the notes can be organized and expressed in a more concise way for final presentation.

Teams often organize a storyboard according to the steps in the improvement process they use (for example, Plan-Do-Study-Act). The following storyboard components are logical elements for a storyboard, although not the only way a storyboard can be organized:

- **Project and reason selected.** These first two sections should be filled in at the team's first meeting. Give a brief description of the project in the first box and summarize the issues that led to its selection in the second. Be sure this section explains the project's relevance to the customer.

- **Situation analysis.** This section should summarize what the team knows about the process or problem being addressed at the beginning of the project; it should be completed during or shortly after the team's first meeting. This is a good place to display a flowchart and/or cause-and-effect diagram.

- **Data collection and analysis.** In these sections the team should display charts and graphs that represent data the team has collected and show any conclusions the team has reached. Include check sheets, Pareto charts, run charts, or other data display tools that make this information easy to understand.

- **Goals and actions.** You may want to make room in the storyboard to include a brief description of the goal of each new phase in the project. The following section would then summarize the action steps taken during that phase.

- **Evaluation.** Present the team's conclusions and results of the project. Be sure to include what actions and decisions were most and least effective, and list recommendations for follow-up actions and areas for further improvement. You may want to show a "before and after" comparison here or use other appropriate charts or diagrams.

Benefits

Documenting a team's activities through storyboarding has numerous benefits, not the least of which is that it is an engaging way to keep the team focused and on track. Using storyboards for informal or formal presentations is an excellent way for teams to sharpen presentation skills and get valuable feedback and recognition from colleagues and managers. Also, displaying a storyboard gives others the chance to learn about the improvement process and apply it to new areas; this kind of exposure will help make quality improvement an integral part of the organization's culture.

BASIC COMPONENTS OF A STORYBOARD

- Project
- Reason Selected
- Situation Analysis
- Data Collection
- Data Analysis
- Goals
- Actions
- Evaluation

Examples

- Figure 3-9 shows one format for a storyboard that uses the FOCUS-PDCA© process to guide documentation of team activities.

- Figures 3-10 and 3-11 show a simple format for a storyboard. For each improvement project, the storyboard provides information on the following: departments involved, project definition, changes and enhancements to the process, monitoring information, important functions and dimensions of performance, measure of success, and team members. Thus, this format provides, at a glance, some of the basic information on *what* the project is, *who* is implementing the project, *how* the team has improved the process, and *what* has been accomplished. These two figures shows storyboards for improvement projects related to total knee replacement and C-section response time.

- Figure 3-12 offers a storyboard for a project to improve laboratory cerebrospinal fluid (CSF) processing. This format, more detailed than those of the previous storyboards, uses both words and graphics to demonstrate a team's activities and accomplishments. Two flowcharts dramatically show how the process was simplified, while the run charts clearly show the resulting decrease in number of problems related to CSF processing.

TIPS FOR SUCCESSFUL STORYBOARD CONSTRUCTION

- Don't wait until the project is over to think about storyboarding; make it an ongoing part of the process.
- Use storyboards for both formal and informal presentations to make others aware of your team's activities.
- Include the names of team members so that they gain deserved recognition.
- Make storyboards simple and attractive.
- Ask for feedback and use it.
- Feel free to be creative.

Other Tools for Teams

A few other tools can be helpful to teams. Figure 3-13 (page 63) is a sample request to start an improvement team. Not all improvement efforts are initiated by leaders; often, staff see an opportunity for improvement that they want to address. Staff should have some means of requesting that an improvement team be formed. This request form is one means of doing that.

Figure 3-14 (pages 64–65) offers a list of questions and suggestions that teams can use to make sure their improvement efforts stay on track. This worksheet follows the PDCA process and prompts team members to assess their progress and to spot any gaps in their efforts.

Figure 3-15 (page 66) is another self-assessment tool for teams. This simple check list will be valuable early in an improvement effort to ensure that the effort has a clear purpose and does not duplicate the efforts of others.

Request to Start a Quality Improvement Team (QIT)

Directions: If you are interested in starting a QIT, please send the completed form to:

Date submitted:

Name: ______________________________ Work phone: ____________________
Job title: ____
Department/area: ____
Address—Bldg: ____________________ Room: ____________ Box: __________
Supervisor: ______________________ Work phone: ____________________

1. Briefly describe the current problem or opportunity for improvement:

____

____

2. How does the problem impact any of the following areas?

a) the quality of a product or service: ____________________________

____

____

b) customer satisfaction: _______________________________________

____

____

c) working environment: ____

____

____

d) cost-effectiveness: ____

____

____

e) other: ____

____

____

____

Figure 3-13 *Staff can use this form to request a charter for an improvement team. Such a form is part of a process to keep track of improvement efforts throughout the organization and to set priorities among those efforts.*

Source: Creps LB, Oxford A, Vegeda PR: Performance improvement review: Implementation of total quality in medical information services. *Top Health Inf Manage* 14(2):65, 1993.© 1993 Aspen Publishers, Inc.

A Plan-Do-Check-Act Worksheet

1. What are we trying to accomplish?

Some questions to consider: (a) What is our aim? (b) What need is tied to that aim? What exactly do we know about that need? (c) What is the process we are working on? (d) What is the link between our aim and this process? Does this process offer us the most leverage for work in support of our aim? (e) What background information do we have available about this improvement—customer, other?

2. How will we know that change is an improvement?

Some questions to consider: (a) Who are the customers? What would constitute improvement in their eyes? (b) What is the output of the process? (c) How does the process work? (d) How does the process currently vary?

3. What changes can we ask that we predict will lead to improvement?

Some questions to consider: (a) Reflecting on the process described, are there ideas for improvement that come readily to mind? (b) Would a simple decision matrix help you decide which to work on first? (c) Are all our decision criteria worded to make their scoring in the same direction? (d) For the change we'd like to try, what is our prediction? (e) What questions do we have about the change, the process, and our prediction? What will you need to check? Do these questions help us link to the overall aim and need?

4. How shall we PLAN the pilot?

Some questions to consider: (a) Who is going to do what, by when, where, and how? (b) Is the "owner" of the process involved? (c) How shall we measure to answer our questions—to confirm or reject our prediction?

Figure 3-14 *This worksheet helps teams or work groups through the Plan-Do-Check-Act improvement process. The worksheet poses key questions to be answered.*

Source: Batalden PB, Stoltz PK: A framework for the continual improvement of health care: Building and applying professional and improvement knowledge to test changes in daily work. *Jt Comm J Qual Improv* 19(10):446–447, 1993. Worksheet developed with the help of Tom Nolan, PhD, of Associates in Process improvement. ©1992 HCA Quality Resource Group, Jun 1993. Used with permission.

A Plan-Do-Check-Act Worksheet, *continued*

5. What are we learning as we DO the pilot?

Some questions to consider: (a) What have we learned from our planned pilot and collection of information? (b) What have we learned from the unplanned information we collect? (c) Was the pilot congruent with the plan?

6. As we CHECK and study what happened, what have we learned?

Some questions to consider: (a) Was our prediction correct? (b) Did the pilot work better for all types of customers—or just some of them? (c) What did we learn about planning the next change?

7. As we ACT to hold the gains or abandon our pilot efforts, what needs to be done?

Some questions to consider: (a) What should be standardized? (b) What training should be considered to provide continuity? (c) How should continued monitoring be undertaken? (d) If the pilot efforts should be abandoned, what has been learned?

8. Looking back over the whole pilot, what have we learned?

Some questions to consider: (a) What was learned that we expected to learn? (b) What unanticipated things did we learn? (c) What did we learn about our predictive ability? (d) Who might be interested in learning what we've learned?

Project Checklist for Teams

	Yes	No
Have you flowcharted the process?	☐	☐
Is this something within your team's span of control?	☐	☐
Do you have a member from each part of the process?	☐	☐
Have you checked to see if other teams are working on something similar?	☐	☐
Have you developed ground rules that everyone agrees to?	☐	☐
Have you selected a team leader and a team facilitator?	☐	☐
Do all team members understand their roles?	☐	☐
Have you done a commitment analysis?	☐	☐
Do you know where to go to get help?	☐	☐
Will everyone be able to see the results?	☐	☐
What will the project cost?	☐	☐
What will it save?	☐	☐

Figure 3-15 *This checklist is designed to help improvement teams ensure that they can effectively address the process they plan to tackle.*

Source: ©1993 Organizational Learning Group, Mount Pleasant, SC. Used with permission.

References

1. Scholtes PR: *The Team Handbook.* Madison, WI: Joiner Associates, Inc, 1992, pp 4–14.
2. Hospital Corporation of America (HCA) Quality Resource Group: *Hospitalwide Quality Technology Network.* Nashville, TN: HCA, 1991, pp 19–22.

Section 4

Tools for Data Collection

Data are essential to any improvement effort. Without accurate data about how a process performs, it is not possible to find areas needing improvement. Similarly, if data show problems in the way a process performs, more data are necessary to help determine the causes behind that performance. Finally, data are needed to measure the effect of any improvement action.

Although data must be analyzed to give teams the information they need, the first step is collecting the data. The tools in this section are designed to help you collect the data you need. This section focuses on the two key tools: indicators, which help define which data to collect, and check sheets and other forms used to collect data related to the indicators.

Indicators

Indicators are quantitative measures of a specific part of a process or of an outcome. More specifically, they can be related to one or more dimensions of performance, including efficacy, appropriateness, availability, timeliness, effectiveness, continuity, safety, efficiency, and respect and caring. Indicators, by themselves, do not directly measure quality. Rather, they help provide data that, when analyzed, give information about quality. By providing the means for objective data collection, indicators direct attention to potential performance issues that may require further investigation.

Indicators should be created when a team needs baseline data about how a process is performing. Indicators are also used when a decision has been made to improve a process. At this stage, indicators facilitate measurement that should lead to detailed information about how a process is performing. And indicators are used to demonstrate the effects of a particular improvement action. Indicators are essential for all data collection and are required for each of the statistical tools in this book.

Types of Indicators

Indicators can be divided into two general categories: *sentinel-event* indicators and *aggregate-data* indicators.

A *sentinel-event indicator* records an event that is significant enough to trigger further investigation each time it occurs. These events are well known in risk management, and they usually are undesirable and occur infrequently. Some examples of sentinel-event indicators are

- intrahospital mortality of patients within two postprocedure days of procedures involving anesthesia administration, and
- intrahospital maternal deaths occurring within 42 days postpartum.

Sentinel-event indicators are important to use because of the seriousness of the events they measure. But they are not as effective in measuring the overall quality of a process as other indicators because eliminating these extremes may not significantly alter the average level of performance.

Aggregate-data indicators measure many events. The aggregation of data may be reported in one of two ways—as a continuous variable or as a rate-based (discrete) variable.

Continuous-variable indicators. Each value of a continuous-variable indicator is a precise measurement that can fall anywhere along a continuous scale. An example is the number of days from surgery to discharge of patients undergoing isolated coronary artery bypass graft procedures.

Rate-based indicators. The value of a measurement of a rate-based indicator reflects the frequency of an event or condition and is expressed as a proportion or a ratio. A *proportion* shows the number of occurrences over the entire group within which the occurrence could take place (for example, patients delivered by cesarean section over all deliveries). A *ratio* shows occurrences compared with a different but related phenomenon (for example, ventilated inpatients who develop pneumonia over inpatient ventilator days).

Use of Indicators

Indicators should be tailored specifically to the functions or processes they are measuring. When selecting a process to measure, consider those that are important to the organization, frequently performed, and prone to problems. Processes that pose a high risk for patients (or staff) also are good candidates. Once the process has been selected, indicators can be developed to measure the process. The nonstatistical tools explained in this book (brainstorming, affinity diagrams, multivoting, selection grids, and flowcharts) help teams identify appropriate processes and indicators.

Often, existing data sources can suggest viable indicators. That is, the team can use data already being collected for another purpose to measure a process. A helpful early step in preparation for measurement is to compile an inventory of existing sources (such as reports, logs, and computer summaries) that contain data relevant to the process to be measured.

Indicators should be phrased as complete and objective statements that can be answered with a specific measurement or indication of whether the event in question occurred. The validity and reliability of all data and subsequent data displays depend on the clarity and specificity of your indicators. (Validity refers to the degree to which an indicator identifies events meriting further review; reliability refers to the accuracy with which an indicator identifies occurrences from among the potential cases.) There must be no room for individual interpretation during data collection. Teams may want to consult an expert in statistics and/or performance measurement to make sure that the selected indicators are feasible. After the indicators are selected, tools such as check sheets can be used to collect the data (see pages 73–78), and tools such as run charts can be used to display the findings (see Section 5, pages 79–83).

For a more detailed treatment of indicators, refer to the *Primer on Indicator Development and Application*, available from the Joint Commission.

Benefits of Indicator Use

Identifying indicators and collecting the relevant data are essential steps toward understanding why a process performs the way it does. Indicators allow you to conduct detailed, objective measurement, which allows objective assessment, which leads to possibilities for improvement. Indicators help you establish a performance database that serves as a history of performance against which to judge the results of your improvement efforts. Once a process is functioning at the desired levels, continued measurement based on indicators should be used to help ensure that improvement is maintained.

Examples

Consider the following example of an indicator related to obstetric care:

$$\frac{\textit{Patients with vaginal birth after cesarean section (VBAC)}}{\textit{Patients delivered with a history of previous cesarean section}}$$

This indicator could be used to evaluate prenatal patient evaluation, education, and treatment selection. For example, if measurement using this indicator showed a VBAC rate higher than regional or national averages, further measurement and assessment might show the need to better evaluate a patient's suitability for VBAC, to change patient education processes and materials to help patients understand the viability of VBACs, and/or to change physicians' practice patterns regarding VBACs.

Table 4-1 (below) lists several other possible indicators pertaining to acute inpatient care. Table 4-2 (page 71) shows a format useful for developing effective indicators.

Table 4-1 Examples of Indicators for Acute Inpatient Care*

Live-born infants with a birth weight less than 2,500 grams
———
Number of after-hours service calls during the last quarter

Patients with principal discharge diagnosis of congestive heart failure (CHF) with documented etiology
———
Patients with principal discharge diagnosis of CHF

Patients undergoing percutaneous transluminal coronary angioplasty: number of days from procedure to discharge

Intrahospital mortality of patients with a principal discharge diagnosis of acute myocardial infarction (AMI)
———
Patients with a principal discharge diagnosis of AMI

Patients undergoing resection for primary cancer of the colon or rectum whose preoperative evaluation by a managing physician included examination of the entire colon
———
Patients undergoing resection for primary cancer of the colon or rectum

Trauma patients undergoing selected abdominal surgical procedures: time from emergency department arrival to procedure

Inpatients 65 years of age or older in whom creatine clearance has been estimated
———
Inpatients 65 years of age or older

Inpatients: number of prescribed medications at discharge

Selected inpatient and outpatient surgical procedures complicated by a surgical site infection
———
Number of selected inpatient and outpatient surgical procedures

**These indicators are selected from the Joint Commission's Indicator Measurement System. The full list of indicators is found in Appendix C of the* 1996 Comprehensive Accreditation Manual for Hospitals.

Table 4-2 Indicator Development Form Format

I. Indicator Statement

II. Definition of Terms

Define terms contained in the indicator that need further explanation for data collection purposes.

III. Type of Indicator

A. Indicate whether this indicator is

1. _____ a rate-based indicator, or

2. _____ a sentinel event indicator.

B. Indicate whether this indicator primarily addresses

1. _____ a process of care, or

2. _____ an outcome of care.

IV. Rationale

A. Explain why this indicator is useful and the specific process or outcome that will be monitored.

B. Identify supportive references used to develop the above rationale.

C. Identify the components of quality that are assessed by this indicator.

V. Description of Indicator Population

A. Indicator numerator:
____
Indicator denominator:

B. Subcategories (identify patient subpopulations by which the indicator data will be separated for analysis.)

VI. Indicator Data Collection Logic

A. List the data elements and corresponding data sources from which data elements may be retrieved.

B. Describe the sequence of data element aggregation through which the numerator events and denominator events are identified by the indicator.

VII. Underlying Factors

List factors that may explain variation in indicator data and thereby direct quality improvement activities.

A. Patient factors (factor outside the health care organization's control contributing to patient outcomes):

1. Severity of illness (factors related to the degree of illness or stage of disease prior to treatment).

2. Comorbid conditions (disease factors, not intrinsic to the primary disease, that may influence the frequency of the event identified by the indicator.

3. Other patient factors (nondisease factors that may have an impact on the frequency of the event, such as age, sex, refusal to consent).

B. Practitioner factors (factors, usually controllable by the organization, related to specific practitioners, for example, nurses, physicians, respiratory therapists).

C. Organization factors (factors, usually controllable by the organization, that contribute to either specific aspects of patient care or to the general ability of caregivers to provide services).

REVIEW: TYPES OF INDICATORS

- **Aggregate-data indicator.** A performance measure based on collection and aggregation of data about many events.
    - —**Continuous-variable indicator**. A type of aggregate-data indicator. The value of each measurement can fall anywhere along a continuous scale.
    - —**Rate-based indicator.** A type of aggregate-data indicator. The value of each measurement is expressed as a proportion or as a ratio.
- **Sentinel-event indicator**. A performance measure that identifies an individual event that is serious enough to *always* trigger further evaluation.

KEY CHARACTERISTICS OF AN INDICATOR

- Expressed in quantitative terms (units of measurement)
- Relates directly to a specific part of a process or outcome
- Identifies events that merit review
- Accurately and completely identifies occurrences

POINTS TO REMEMBER

- Tailor indicators specifically to processes that are important to the organization; those that are frequently performed, high risk, and/or prone to problems are good candidates.
- Use brainstorming, multivoting, selection grids, affinity diagrams, and flowcharts to help identify appropriate processes and indicators.
- Review existing data sources and list the important events seen in each source to help in drafting indicators.
- Be sure that indicators are phrased as complete and objective statements; leave no room for interpretation.
- Consult an expert in statistics, if feasible.

Check Sheets

A check sheet is a simple tool that shows how often an event or condition occurs. It is the most basic statistical tool, used to record data that answer objective statements requiring a simple yes or no response (indicators).

Check sheets are used at the beginning of the data collection and analysis process, when a team needs to gather preliminary data to measure a process and detect its patterns. The information gathered with a check sheet provides the foundation for the more complex statistical tools explained in Section 5.

Process

A check sheet must be specifically tailored to the process or outcome being studied. The following steps can be used to create a check sheet:

1. **Agree on the data to be collected.** A team may decide to collect data to provide a baseline for how a process performs. Or the team may want to collect data about problem areas uncovered in a flowchart. Or perhaps the team wants to investigate how often the causes identified in a cause-and-effect diagram occur. At this stage, the team also should consider the source of the data: Will the information be found in existing records, or will it have to be observed firsthand?

2. **Decide who will collect the data and when.** Data collectors must be knowledgeable enough about the process in question to reliably collect the information; they may record the data as part of their normal activities or do it separately. The team also must decide how much data to collect. Will the collection take place during a period of hours, days, or weeks? Make sure to collect enough data so that the information is reliable. Decide whether data will be collected during all shifts or during days only or evenings only, and consider the effects of collecting data during particular months or days of the week.

3. **Select a sample size, if appropriate.** Some events occur with such high volume that recording every relevant situation is impractical. If this is the case, the team may need to select a random, representative sample of at least 20%. It is crucial that the sample be statistically reliable. If the team must select a sample, it should consult an expert or a textbook on statistics.

4. **Phrase the statement (indicator).** It is important to phrase the subject of data collection as a complete, objective statement that can be answered with a clear yes or no. For the data to be

reliable, everyone must be looking for the same thing; there should be no room for interpretation. "Delayed presurgery waiting time," for example, is much too subjective. This statement could be rephrased as "More than 30 minutes spent in presurgical holding area."

5. **Design the check sheet.** Ideally, those who will collect the data should help design the check sheet. It should be clear and easy to use. Include a place for the date, time, name of data collector, and comments, and leave plenty of space for entering the data. Figure 4-1 (below) shows a generic check sheet format.

6. **Test the sheet.** One way to test a check sheet is to have one or two people who did not help design the sheet use it. Make any necessary improvements to the form based on their feedback.

7. **Distribute the check sheet and collect the data.** Once the format is final, distribute copies to all data collectors; they will then collect data until the end of the specified period. Make certain that collection is done consistently and accurately.

Generic Check Sheet

August 9–15, 1995

Day / Event	Sun	Mon	Tue	Wed	Thu	Fri	Sat
#1	II	𝍸 II	III	IIII	III	𝍸	
#2	I	II	II	IIII	III	𝍸	III
#3	III	I	II	II	III	I	𝍸
#4	IIII	II	I	I	III	II	𝍸
#5	II	𝍸	𝍸	𝍸 I	III	IIII	III
#6	III	III	II	I	III	IIII	II
#7	II	I	III	III	𝍸	III	I
#8	II	III	I	III	IIII	II	I

Figure 4-1 *This format allows staff members to mark how many times a particular event occurs during successive days over a specified period.*

8. **Tally all individual data sheets.** Use a single sheet to tally all information from the individual check sheets. The totals may be aggregated by day, shift, week, month, or occurrence.

9. **Evaluate the data.** At the end of the collection period, the team should examine the results, looking for areas that require further attention. The tools that are described in Section 5 will help the team take the data beyond its raw form so that it can draw conclusions and take action.

Benefits

Check sheets provide a clear record of data gathered about a process or an outcome. Properly acquired, this information will serve as a reliable foundation on which a team can base its other diagnostic activities, which may include surveys and interviews as well as improvement efforts.

Examples

- Figure 4-2 (page 76) shows examples of two check sheets that could be used to collect data about outpatient department delays. The first check sheet allows data collectors to indicate waiting times (in five-minute intervals) for different types of patients. The second check sheet uses a similar format for recording waiting time for three activities involved in an outpatient visit.
- Figure 4-3 (page 77) shows a check sheet that may be used to indicate the cause of delays in physical therapy treatment. This detailed data-collection tool offers a broad range of causes and subcauses of delay and allows the data collector to check the relevant cause of each incident.
- The format shown in Figure 4-4 (page 78) allows the data collector to create a simple bar chart by placing checks above the appropriate finding in a vertical column. This sheet includes easy-to-understand instructions and a clear indicator statement regarding missing medical records.

REVIEW OF PROCEDURE

1. Agree on the data to be collected.
2. Decide who will collect the data and when.
3. Select a sample size, if appropriate.
4. Phrase the statement (indicator).
5. Design the check sheet.
6. Test the sheet.
7. Distribute the check sheet and collect the data.
8. Tally all individual data sheets.
9. Evaluate the data.

Check Sheet Formats: Outpatient Department Delays

Outpatient Waiting Time—Patient Type

Patient Waiting Time (minutes)	5	10	15	20+
Prescheduled with outpatient department	~~IIII~~ IIII	~~IIII~~ I	IIII	I
Prescheduled and preregistered	II	I	I	
Walk-in (no advance notice)		~~IIII~~ ~~IIII~~ II	~~IIII~~ ~~IIII~~ ~~IIII~~ ~~IIII~~	~~IIII~~ ~~IIII~~ ~~IIII~~ ~~IIII~~

Outpatient Waiting Time–by Activity—Walk-ins Only

Patient Waiting Time (minutes)	5	10	15	20	25	30	35
Registration Preprocedure	~~IIII~~	~~IIII~~	~~IIII~~	~~IIII~~	~~IIII~~	~~IIII~~	~~IIII~~
During the procedure	~~IIII~~	~~IIII~~	IIII				
Postprocedure (cashier)	IIII						

Figure 4-2 *These two formats show how check sheets can be used to record findings for a continuous-variable indicator—in these examples, the amount of time patients wait in the outpatient department.*

Source: ©1991, Roey Kirk Associates, Miami, FL. Used with permission.

Checklist: Physical Therapy Treatment Delays

Category	Cause						
1. Patient unavailable	A. not in room						
	B. meals						
	C. visitors						
	D. phone call						
	E. bathroom						
	F. code/emergency						
	G. another treatment						
2. Interrupted treatment	A. physician						
	B. nurse						
	C. ancillary service						
	D. phone call						
	E. bathroom						
3. Inadequate training of staff							
4. Lack of staff							
5. Communication problem	A. ward clerk						
	B. nursing						
	C. patient						
	D. physical therapy staff						
6. Scheduling problem	A. physical therapy staff						
	B. nursing floor						
	C. patient						
7. Chart not available	A. physician						
	B. other						
8. Decreased medical status of patient							
9. Transfer to ICU, CCU, or surgery							
10. Patient on isolation preventing treatment							
11. Equipment unavailable	A. not in stock						
	B. in use						
	C. not working						
	D. out of service						
	E. staff not trained						
	F. forgot to take						

12. Other ______________________________

____

Therapist: ______________________________

Date: ______________________________

Figure 4-3 *This format allows data collectors to record a wide range of events, each of which is a potential cause of delay in physical therapy. The causes are grouped into categories such as "patient unavailable" and "lack of staff." If, for example, a team had created a cause-and-effect diagram and wanted to determine the frequency of those causes, this checklist would be an ideal tool.*

Source: West Paces Medical Center, Atlanta, 1992. Used with permission.

Check Sheet: Missing Medical Records

MISSING MEDICAL RECORDS STUDY

Instructions

- Mark an X at the top of this form for each patient seen.
- Ask "Were you at the primary care clinic today?"
- If yes, mark the appropriate place in the bottom of this form.

Specialty: Cardiology **Date:** January 12

Total patients seen today

X X X X X X X X X X X X X X X X X X X X X X X X X X

For "same day" appointment patients:

record present	**no record**
X	
X	
Edwards Rd. Clinic	

record present	**no record**
X	
X	
X	
X	X
Edgewood Ave. Clinic	

record present	**no record**
X	
X	
X	
X	X
South St. Clinic	

Figure 4-4 *This vertical check sheet of events can be used to collect data and to display those data as a bar graph.*

Source: ©1995 Paul E. Plsek & Associates. Used with permission.

Section 5 Tools for Data Analysis

After a team collects data about a process, those data need to be analyzed. Often, data analysis involves some form of comparison—comparison between current findings and previous findings, for example, or comparison between current findings and established standards, critical path specification, or "best practices."

The tools in this section help present data in a way that facilitates analysis. The tools included are run charts, control charts, histograms, and scatter diagrams. These are statistical tools, but not all of them require advanced statistical knowledge.

Run Charts

A run chart is a familiar tool to health care professionals. This type of chart plots points on a graph to show levels of performance over time. The purpose of a run chart is to identify trends and other patterns in a process, including movement away from the average or whether a target level has been attained (and maintained). This kind of information helps teams understand how a process is working and identify which areas are in need of improvement and when conditions are improving.

A run chart is used during the problem-identification, data-analysis, and result-evaluation phases of the improvement process, or any time a team needs a simple visual display of performance trends over a specific period of time.

Process

A run chart is one of the simplest tools to construct and use. Creating a run chart involves the following steps:

1. **Decide what the chart will measure.** The first step is to determine what data will be collected and over what period of time. For instance, a team may decide to measure the number of confirmed adverse drug reactions

per month or the laboratory turnaround time for stat test orders. The data used should encompass a time period long enough to show a trend.

2. **Draw the graph's axes.** The horizontal (x) axis should indicate time or sequence, and the vertical (y) axis should indicate what is being studied, in increments, as shown in Figure 5-1 (below). Be sure to clearly mark all units of measurement on the chart.

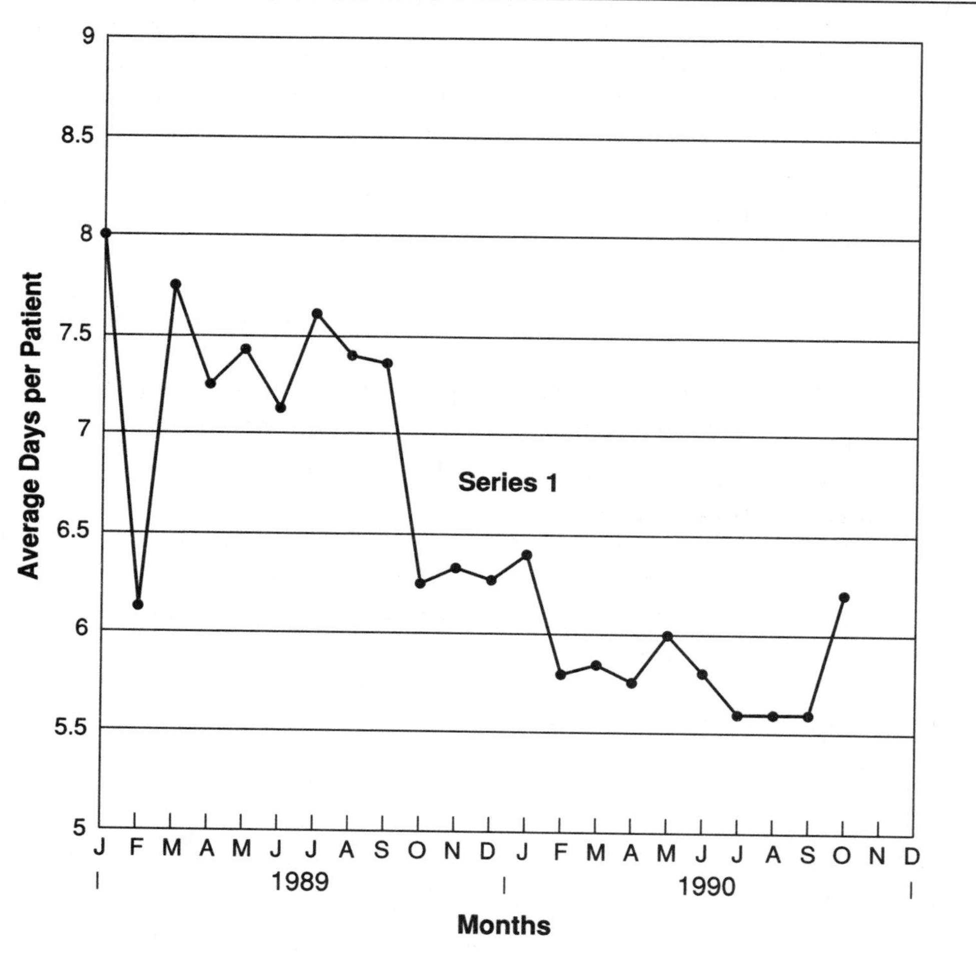

Figure 5-1 *This figure shows how a run chart is used to display levels of performance over time—in this case, the average length of stay per patient over two years.*

3. **Plot the data points and connect them with a line.** Plot the correct measurement for each point in time. Be absolutely sure to keep data in the same sequence in which they were collected. When all the points are plotted, connect them with a line, which will help anyone viewing the chart to easily spot performance trends and patterns. The team may also want to indicate on the chart any significant changes or events that occur during the time period you are studying. This can be done by drawing and labeling dashed lines through the chart at the appropriate points on the x axis.

4. **Evaluate the chart to identify meaningful trends.** The team may want to seek expert statistical advice for this task. Above all, keep in mind that the purpose of this tool is to help the team focus on trends and patterns in the process; although a single point on the chart may indicate an event worthy of review, the purpose of the chart is to show patterns and trends in performance. The following are some key concepts to consider when analyzing the chart:
   - An equal number of points will fall above and below the average; this is how the average is calculated.
   - A "run" of six or more points on one side of the average indicates a statistically unusual event or a shift in the average.
   - A trend of six or more steadily increasing or decreasing points (with no reversals) also indicates an important change.
   - Annual cycles, such as when most staff take vacations during a year, should also be considered.

5. **Investigate the findings.** Any time the findings indicate a demonstrable trend or pattern, the team should investigate further to determine the cause of movement. If the change or shift represented in the chart is favorable, it should become part of the system. If the shift is unfavorable, the team should eliminate it through actions to improve performance.

Benefits

The ability to spot trends, cycles, and other patterns is crucial to any improvement process. Run charts are simple to create and they present a valuable picture of performance measured over a period of time. They answer the questions, "Is performance static or changing?" and, "If it is changing, is the change for better or worse?"

Examples

- Figure 5-1 shows an example of a run chart used to display average length of stay. The vertical axis indicates number of days, and the horizontal axis indicates the range of time—a two-year period divided by months. As the chart shows, average length of stay dropped from eight days to between five and six days during this period. Although average length of stay dropped to just over six days in only the second month of monitoring, the run chart shows that the *trend* is a slower reduction over time.
- Figure 5-2 (below) shows a variation on a simple run chart. This chart, which displays trends in number of rejected Medicare claims, superimposes three run charts. Each line tracks claims rejected for a specific cause. Thus, the chart allows a team not only to see trends in overall performance, but to begin comparing various causes for that performance.

Run Chart: Rejected Medicare Claims

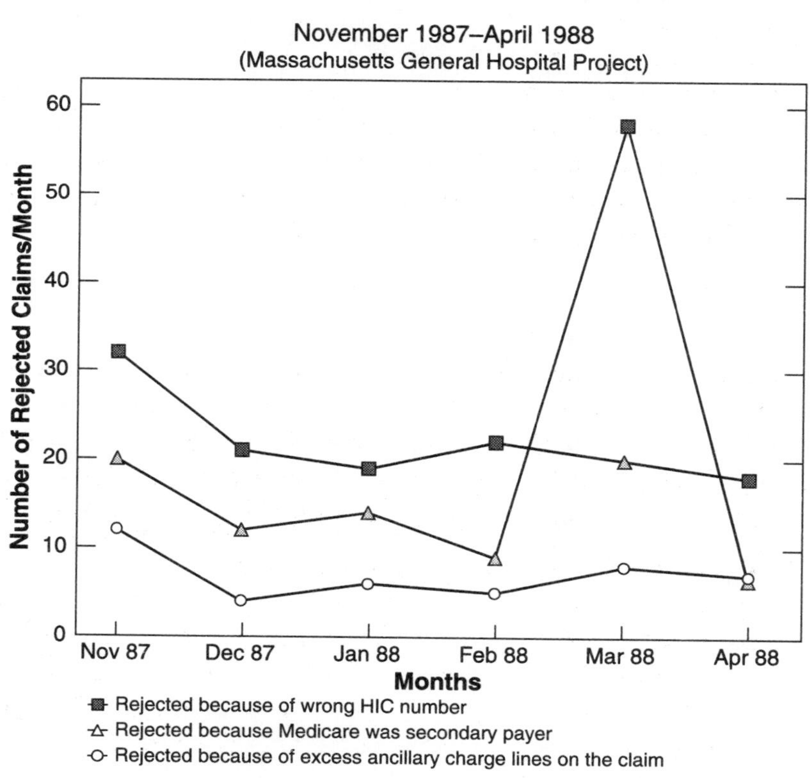

Figure 5-2 *This figure superimposes three run charts to compare three causes of rejected Medicare claims.*

Source: Berwick DM, et al: *Curing Health Care: New Strategies for Quality Improvement*. San Francisco: Jossey-Bass Publishers, 1990, p 125. Used with permission.

REVIEW OF PROCEDURE

1. Decide what the chart will measure.
2. Draw the graph's axes.
3. Plot the data points and connect them with a line.
4. Evaluate the chart to identify meaningful trends.
5. Investigate the findings.

Control Charts

Control charts are run charts that include statistically determined "control" limits on either side of the average or mean. Control charts are designed to show what type of variation exists in a process and whether the process is statistically "in control." A variables control chart measures quantitative data such as time or length, and an attributes control chart measures qualitative data such as an error rate.

Control charts are used to identify problems, analyze data, and evaluate results of an improvement action; they are useful whenever a team needs to know whether the variation in a process is common (inherent in the way the process is designed and performed) or is caused by unique events or individual actions. Generally, control charts are used to track performance over a significant period of time; thus, they may not be appropriate for short-term improvement projects.

Process

Control charts involve complex statistical rules, and it is necessary to consult a textbook, handbook, or other source of statistics expertise to fully understand how to create them. Please see the Appendix to this book, "Constructing Statistical Control Charts," for a more detailed explanation than the basic steps of control chart construction shown here:

1. **Choose a process to evaluate and obtain a data set.** For the purposes of this explanation, we will assume that the team already has studied the process and has obtained a data set of at least 15 to 20 data points using a check sheet or another collection tool. For the steps that follow, it is important that the data were obtained before any adjustments were made to the process.

2. **Calculate the mean.** The *mean* (also called the *average*) of a data set provides a reference point that shows the central tendency of a data distribution. To obtain the mean, divide the sum of all measurements by the total number of measurements in the data set.

3. **Calculate the standard deviation and set upper and lower control limits.** The *standard deviation* of a data set is the measure of its variability. Consult a source of statistics expertise to aid in calculating the standard deviation. Typically, the control limits are one to three times higher or lower than the standard deviation relative to the mean. For example, say the mean is 31 and the standard deviation is 5. If you set control limits at twice the standard deviation (plus or minus 10), the upper control limit would be 41 and the lower limit would be 21.

4. **Create the control chart.** Plot the horizontal and vertical axes the way you would for a run chart. On the chart, plot the mean and the upper and lower control limits. Refer to Figure 5-3 (pages 85–86) to see how the chart should look.

5. **Plot the data.** As is done for a run chart, the next step is to plot the correct measurements for each point in time, remembering to keep the data in the same sequence in which they were collected. Connect the points with a line to show the performance trends and patterns.

6. **Analyze the chart and investigate findings.** First, determine whether the process is statistically in or out of control. A process must be in control before overall performance can be improved. If the data points fall within the control limits, then the causes of variation are considered common (or random) and the process is in control. If points fall above or below the limits, the process is out of control. This means that the variation is caused by special, unpredictable events and the process needs more immediate investigation.

   When a process is out of control, try to determine why.[1] Has there been a significant change in the environment? Were any untrained workers involved in the process at the time? Has there been a change in equipment maintenance? Special causes must be eliminated before the process can be fundamentally improved and before the control chart can be used as a monitoring tool.

7. **Remember that the terms "in control" and "out of control" do not signify whether a process meets the desired level of performance.** These are statistical definitions that refer to whether a process is consistent. A process may be in control, but may be consistently poor in terms of quality, and the converse may be true.

Figure 5-3 shows five examples of patterns or trends that might be shown by a control chart.

Sample Control Charts

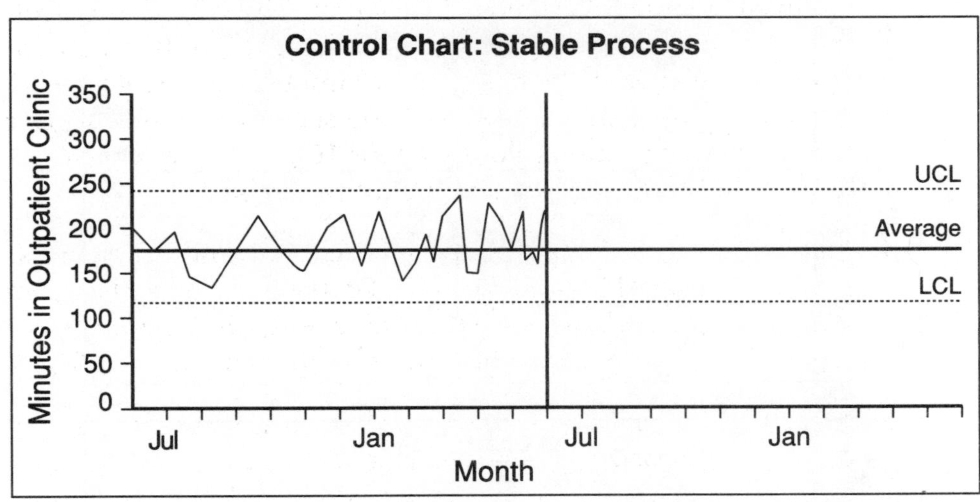

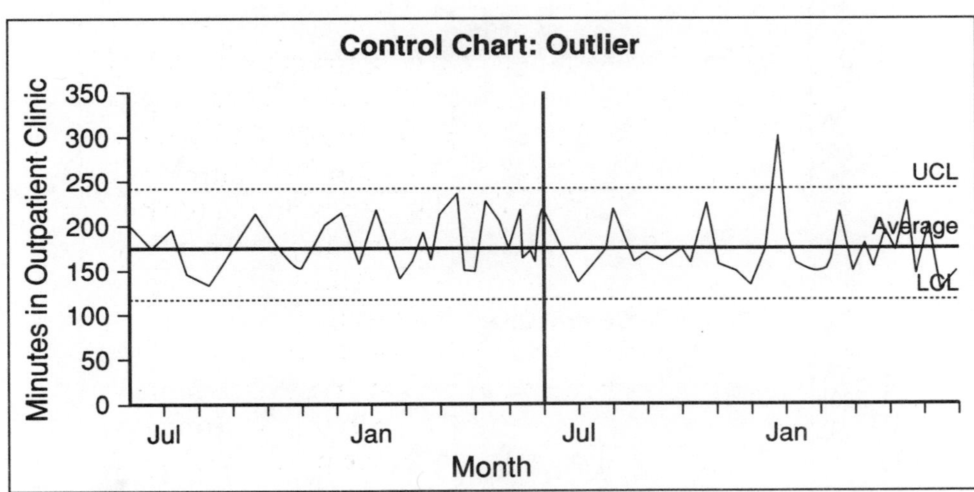

Figure 5-3 *This series of five control charts illustrates different patterns of performance an organization is likely to encounter. A control chart is a run chart with a statistically determined upper control limit (UCL) and lower control limit (LCL). When performance is within those limits, the process is said to be "in control." In control does not mean desirable; rather, it means the process is stable, or not affected by special causes of variation (such as equipment failure). A process must be in control before it can be systematically improved.*

The five figures show the following scenarios:

Stable process. *All points are within the control limits. The process is thus stable or in control.*

Outlier. *One point jumps outside a control limit. Staff should determine whether this single occurrence is likely to recur.*

Sample Control Charts, *continued*

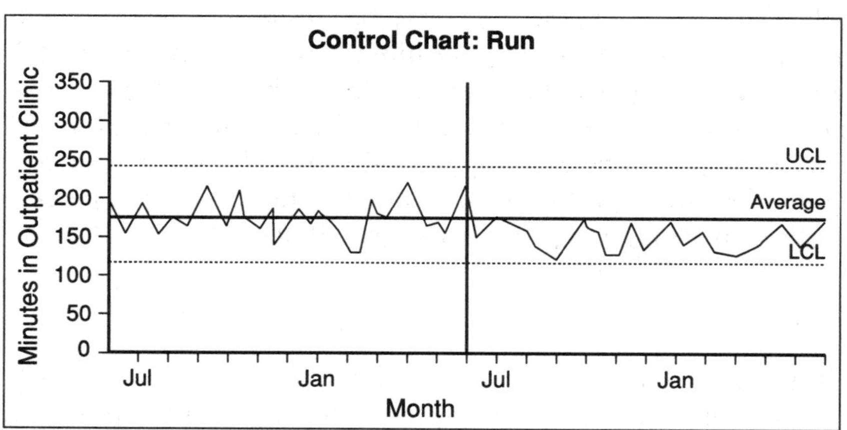

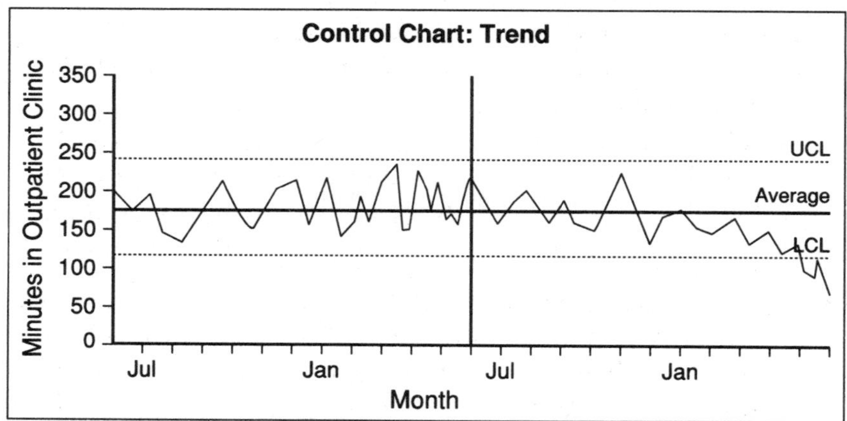

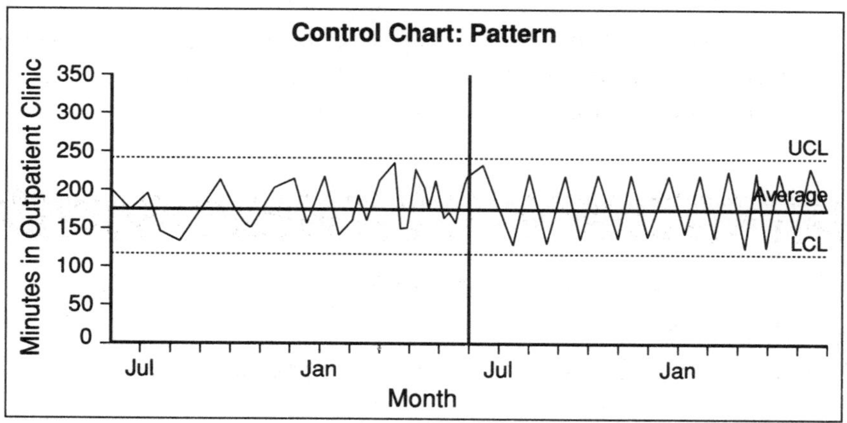

Run. *A run occurs when a given number of points in a row are on one or the other side of the average. This may suggest an opportunity for improvement.*

Trend. *A trend is a steady rise or fall in performance. Trends headed toward or crossing control limits suggest that further assessment is necessary.*

Pattern. *An identifiable pattern in performance such as that shown here may indicate a performance problem associated with factors such as time of day, shift, season, and so forth.*

Benefits

In the early stages of improvement efforts, the "usual" pattern for events in a given process may not be known. Determining the mean will establish baselines and provide an important reference point for future activities. Setting upper and lower limits on a control chart establishes thresholds for evaluation, helps teams determine when opportunity exists for improvement, and stimulates further investigation. After improvements are made, control charts help a team monitor a process and keep it in control.

Examples

- The example in Figure 5-4 (page 88) shows a control chart used to display data about the amount of time between physician order and emergency room discharge for a 10-day period. This chart shows three cases of special-cause variation: days three and five reach the upper control limit, and day nine falls below the lower control limit. The team using this control chart would next investigate what special circumstances might have caused these variations in discharge time. (The team would probably also investigate the circumstances surrounding day seven, which is a statistically significant variation as well.)
- Figure 5-5 (page 88) shows total charge discrepancies in respiratory therapy over a year and a half. This chart shows that the process initially was statistically out of control; note the outlier for August 1989. After the process was statistically brought under control, an improvement initiative resulted in an improvement in overall performance. Thus, the process was stabilized (variation reduced) and brought to a new level, when a different mean, upper control limit, and lower control limit were set.

REVIEW OF PROCEDURE

1. Choose a process to evaluate and obtain a data set.
2. Calculate the mean.
3. Calculate the standard deviation and set upper and lower control limits.
4. Create the control chart.
5. Plot the data.
6. Analyze the chart and investigate findings.
7. Remember that the terms "in control" and "out of control" do not signify whether a process meets the deserved level of performance.

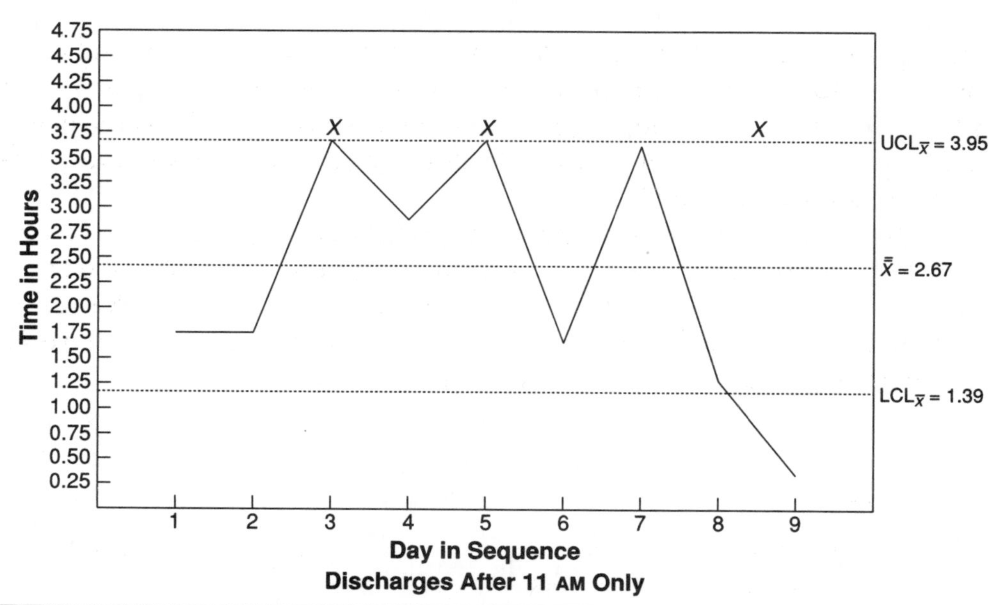

Figure 5-4 *This control chart shows admission process time from physician order to actual emergency room discharge. The upper control limit (UCL) and lower control limit (LCL) represent the limits within which the process is statistically in control.*

Source: Berwick DM et al: *Curing Health Care: New Strategies for Quality Improvement.* San Francisco: Jossey-Bass Publishers, 1990. Used with permission.

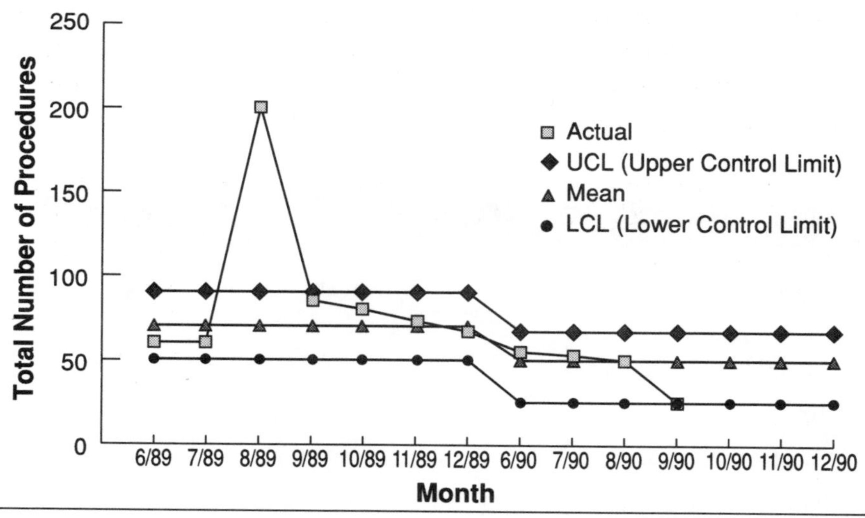

Figure 5-5 *This control chart shows a significant improvement in performance over the duration of a quality improvement team. Once the overall level of performance shifts, the upper and lower control limits are recalculated for the new performance level.*

Source: West Paces Medical Center, Atlanta, 1992. Used with permission.

Histograms

Histograms are bar charts that display patterns of variation in a set of data. They are similar to Pareto charts in form (see Section 6, pages 110–115), but they are not limited in content to attribute data (the characteristics of a product or service). Histograms display the way measurement data are distributed.

Histograms are valuable tools for the data-analysis and result-evaluation stages of performance improvement. They address issues such as how much and what kind of variation exist in a process. By studying the results, a team will be able to determine whether the variation is normal and identify target areas that need further attention.

Process

This process may seem a bit more complex than others. Following these steps carefully will minimize confusion and help a team build an accurate histogram. For more detailed information, a team should consult a statistics handbook or textbook or an individual who is an expert in statistics:

1. **Obtain the data set and count the number of data points.** Collect all the data to be analyzed and count each item as a data point. For example, in the example in Figure 5-6 (page 90) the total number of data points is all cases in which laboratory response time is noted for a given time period.

2. **Determine the range for the entire data set.** Find the largest (62) and smallest (11) values in the data set, and then subtract the smallest value from the largest value. This will give the range ($R = 51$).

3. **Set the number of classes into which the data will be divided.** The classes will make the bars of the histogram. Use the following guide to determine the number of classes (represented by the letter K):[2]

Number of Data Points	Number of Classes (K)
< 50	5–7
51–100	6–10
100–250	7–12
More than 250	10–20

The example in Figure 5-6 has 100 data points and 11 classes.

Histogram: Laboratory Response Time

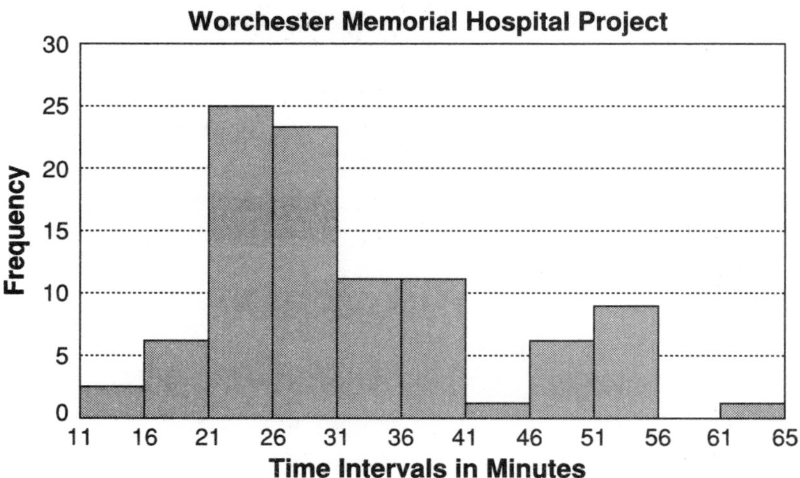

Figure 5-6 *This histogram shows the range of variation in response time from receipt of laboratory specimen, evening shift. The variation is skewed, with a second peak to the right, suggesting that further investigation is warranted.*

Source: Berwick DM, et al: *Curing Health Care: New Strategies for Quality Improvement.* San Francisco: Jossey-Bass Publishers, 1990. Used with permission.

4. **Determine the class width.** To determine how wide each bar will be, divide the range (*R*) by the number of classes (*K*). The resulting number, rounded off, will be the width (*W*) of each class or bar in the histogram. Using this formula, the example's class width is set at 5.

5. **Establish class boundaries.** Class boundaries are the starting and ending points of the bars on the histogram. To establish the boundaries, use the following procedure:

- Take the smallest number in the data set and round it down, if necessary. This number (11 in the example) marks the lower boundary of the first class.
- Add the class width (*W*) to the lower boundary value of the first class. This gives you the lower boundary of the second class (11 + 5 = 16; data set values from 11 to 15 are included in the first class).
- Continue adding the value for *W* to each new value until the lower boundaries for all the classes are established.
- Be sure that the classes are mutually exclusive, so that each data point will fit into one and only one class.

In the example, the classes are as follows:

Class	Includes All Data Set Values from:
1	11 to 15
2	16 to 20
3	21 to 25
4	26 to 30
5	31 to 35
6	36 to 40
7	41 to 45
8	46 to 50
9	51 to 55
10	56 to 60
11	61 to 65

6. **Construct the histogram chart.** Place the values for the classes on the horizontal axis. Along the vertical axis (to the left of the chart) list numbers to represent frequency. Use the example in Figure 5-6 as a guideline for how the chart should look.

7. **Count the data points in each class and create the bars.** Count how many occurrences (how many of the data points) fall into each class, and then create bars of the appropriate height to indicate the frequency of each class on the graph. Refer again to Figure 5-6.

8. **Analyze the findings.** Figure 5-7 (page 92) shows the types of results you are likely to find. In most cases, small variation is ideal, provided it is within specifications. Note the amount of variability, and then check whether the curve made by the tops of the bars is centered at the correct place or if it is skewed. Large variation or skewed distribution may signal that the process requires further attention. Keep in mind, however, that some processes are naturally skewed, and don't expect a "normal" pattern every time.

   In the example in Figure 5-6, the variation shows the need for further attention. The variation is large and skewed to the right. Also, a second peak exists at the eighth and ninth classes. These findings suggest that the variation should be reduced and that further information should be gathered about the response times in the 46-minute to 55-minute ranges. Special conditions may exist for the specimens that require this range of time.

Histograms: Types of Distributions

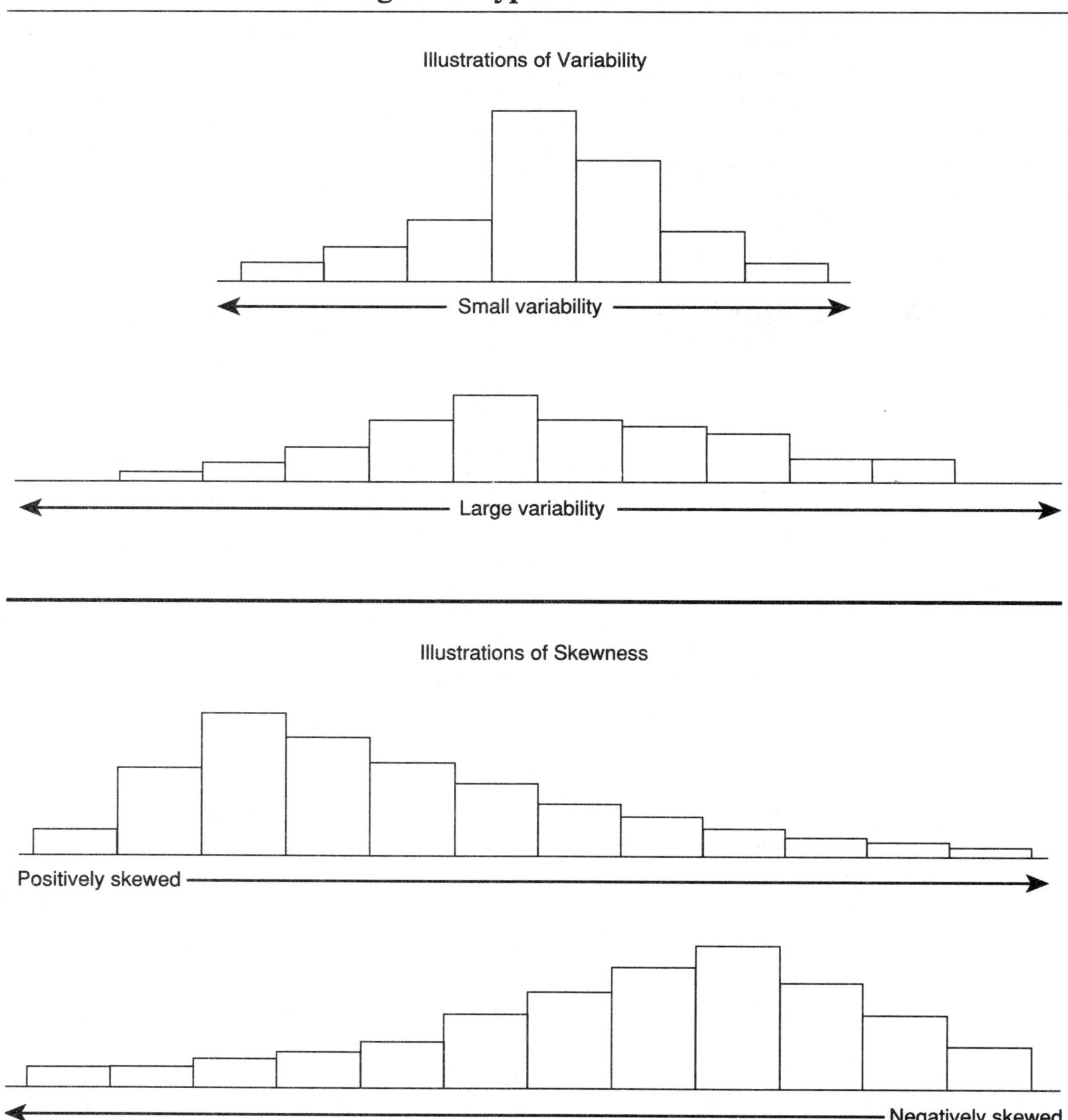

Figure 5-7 *These histograms show four common types of variation distribution: small, large, positively skewed, and negatively skewed. Ideally, distribution is symmetrical and the variation small.*

Source: GOAL/QPC: *The Memory Jogger: A Pocket Guide of Tools for Continuous Improvement.* Methuen, MA: GOAL/QPC, 1988. Used with permission.

Benefits

Histograms are important diagnostic tools because they provide the team with a snapshot of the way data are distributed within a range of values and the amount of variation within a given process. Their easy-to-read format helps a team determine when the process is running high or low and where deviations from specifications occur. This kind of perspective is critical in the improvement process.

Examples

- In Figure 5-8 (below) a histogram indicates the number of physicians needing access to the file room at various times during the day. This histogram shows significant variation and a skewing to the left, indicating the need to change the process to reduce variation.
- The histogram in Figure 5-9 (page 94) addresses the number of days from discharge to "sign date." Each bar represents the frequency with which a certain number of days is taken between discharge and signing the chart.

Histogram: Physician Use of File Room

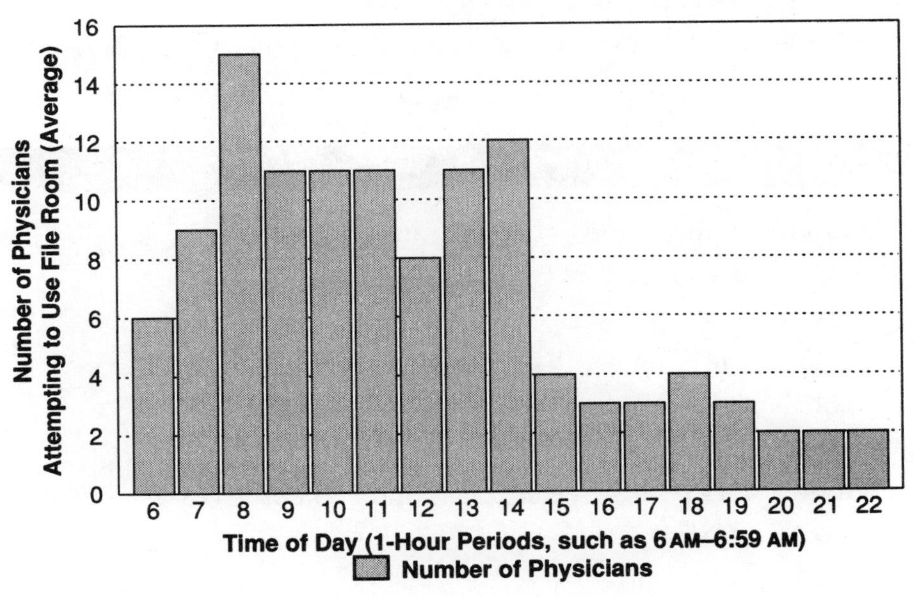

Figure 5-8 *This histogram—showing the number of physicians using the file room at various hours of the day—shows large variation, a skewing to the left, and a second peak between 1 PM and 2 PM.*

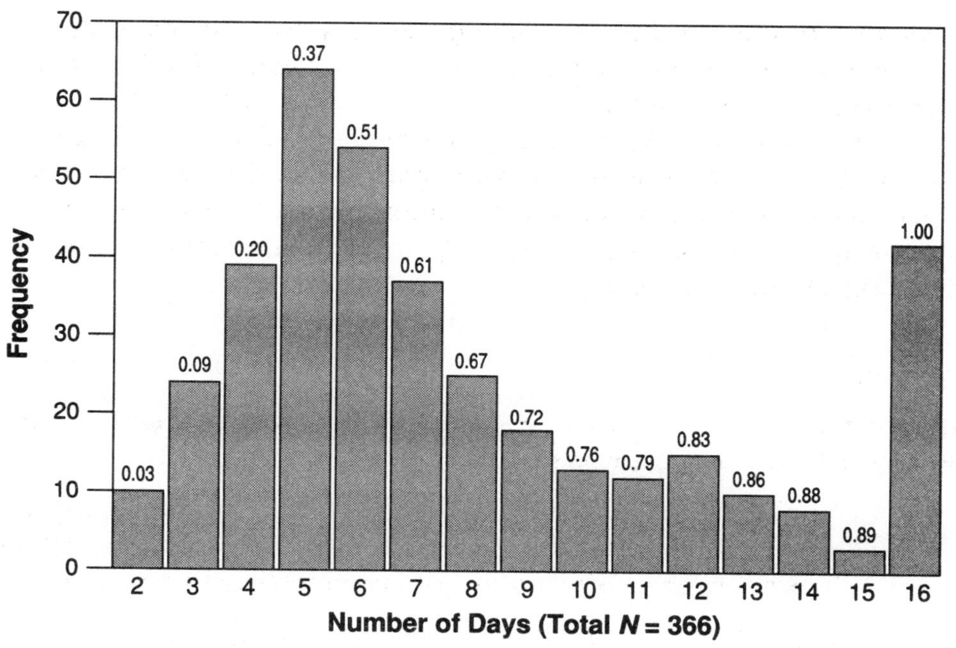

Figure 5-9 *This histogram shows the variation in the number of days that elapse between a patient's discharge and the final signing of the medical record.*

Source: Rush-Presbyterian–St. Luke's Medical Center, Chicago. Used with permission.

REVIEW OF PROCEDURE

1. Obtain the data set and count the number of data points.
2. Determine the range for the entire data set.
3. Set the number of classes into which the data will be divided.
4. Determine the class width.
5. Establish class boundaries.
6. Construct the histogram chart.
7. Count the data points in each class and create the bars.
8. Analyze the findings.

Scatter Diagrams

Scatter diagrams (also called *scattergrams*) are graphs designed to show the statistical correlation (but not necessarily the cause-and-effect relationship) between two variables.

Creating a scatter diagram is appropriate to the data-analysis and result-evaluation phases of the improvement process. Scatter diagrams are used most effectively when a team wants to test a theory about the relationship between two variables, analyze raw data, or monitor an action taken to improve performance.

Process

A team can create a scatter diagram to test the relationship between two variables using the following procedure:

1. **Decide which two variables will be tested.** The team should select two variables it suspects are related (for example, delays in processing tests and total volume of tests to be processed).

2. **Collect and record relevant data.** Gather 50 to 100 paired samples of data involving each of the variables and record them on a data sheet. (This is not the actual construction of the diagram.)

3. **Draw the horizontal and vertical axes.** Usually, the horizontal (x) axis represents the variable you suspect is the cause and the vertical (y) axis, drawn on the left side, is the effect. In this example, the x axis would represent number of delayed tests, and the y axis would represent the total number of tests. Be sure to mark the diagram clearly. Moving up and to the right of each axis, values should increase.

4. **Plot the variables on the graph.** Referring to the data-collection sheet, mark the appropriate intersecting points on the graph. If a value is repeated, circle that point as many times as necessary. (See Figure 5-10, page 96, for an example of a completed scatter diagram.)

5. **Interpret the completed diagram.** Certain conclusions may be drawn according to the way the points cluster on the graph.[3] Remember, if the diagram indicates a relationship, it is not necessarily a cause-and-effect relationship:

   - In general, the more the clusters form a straight line (which could be diagonal), the stronger the relationship between the two variables.

- If points cluster in an area running from lower left to upper right, the two variables have a positive correlation. This means that an increase in *y* may depend on an increase in *x*; if you can control *x*, you have a good chance of controlling *y*.
- If points cluster from upper left to lower right, the variables have a negative correlation. This means that as *x* increases, *y* may decrease. A negative relationship is just as important as a positive relationship.
- If points are scattered all over the diagram, these variables may not have any correlation (the effect, *y*, may be dependent on a variable other than *x*).

Figure 5-11 (page 97) shows several possible patterns, and their meanings, found in scatter diagrams.

Scatter Diagram: Patient Waiting Time Versus Census

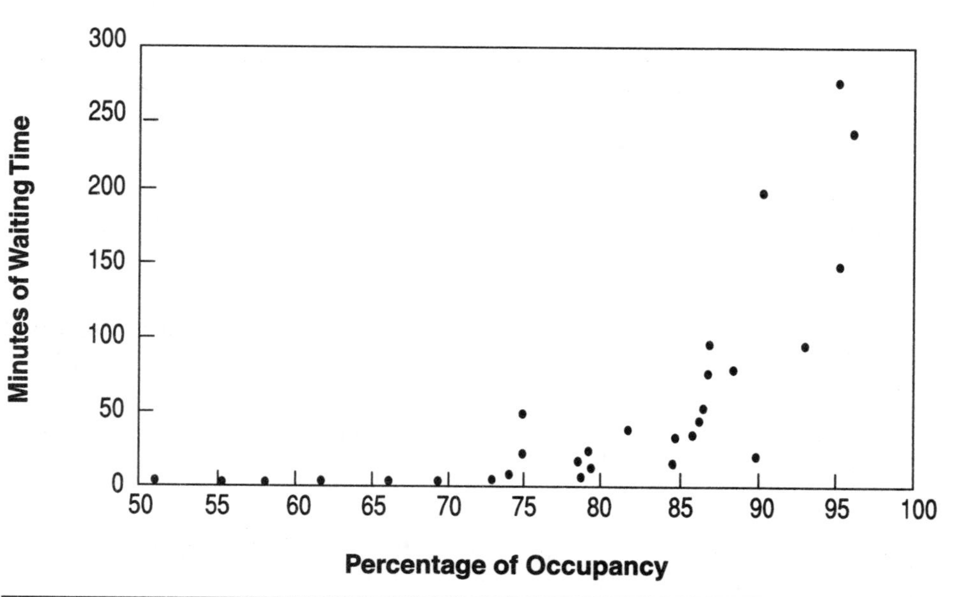

Figure 5-10 *This scatter diagram compares two variables—patient waiting time and hospital occupancy—to determine their relationship. Here, the clustering of points shows that census does affect waiting time.*

Scatter Diagram Findings

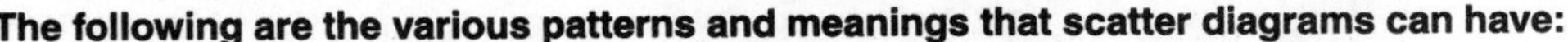

The following are the various patterns and meanings that scatter diagrams can have:

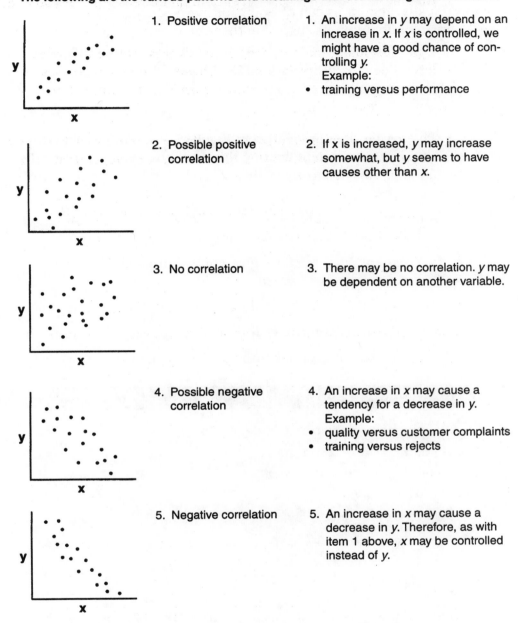

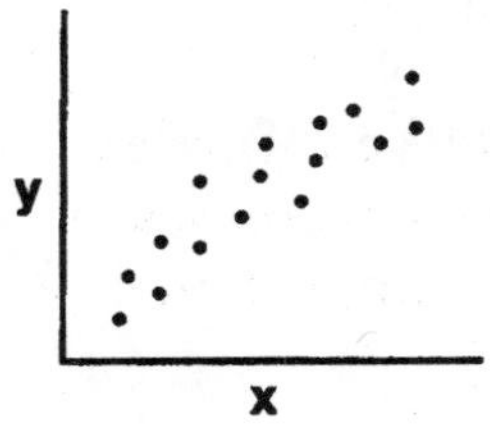

Pattern	Meaning
1. Positive correlation	1. An increase in *y* may depend on an increase in *x*. If *x* is controlled, we might have a good chance of controlling *y*. Example: • training versus performance
2. Possible positive correlation	2. If x is increased, *y* may increase somewhat, but *y* seems to have causes other than *x*.
3. No correlation	3. There may be no correlation. *y* may be dependent on another variable.
4. Possible negative correlation	4. An increase in *x* may cause a tendency for a decrease in *y*. Example: • quality versus customer complaints • training versus rejects
5. Negative correlation	5. An increase in *x* may cause a decrease in *y*. Therefore, as with item 1 above, *x* may be controlled instead of *y*.

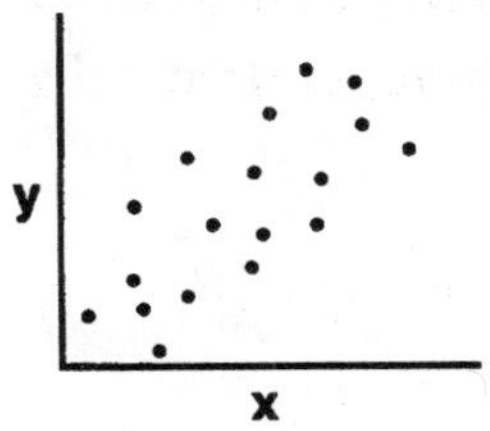

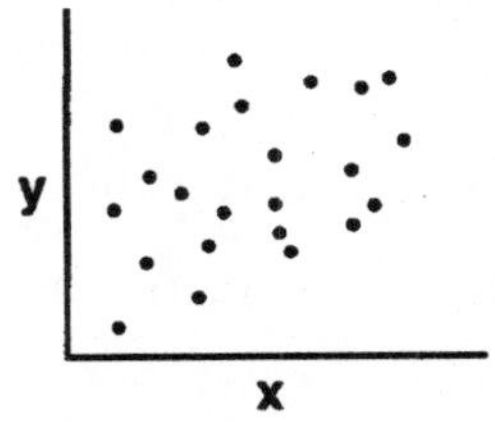

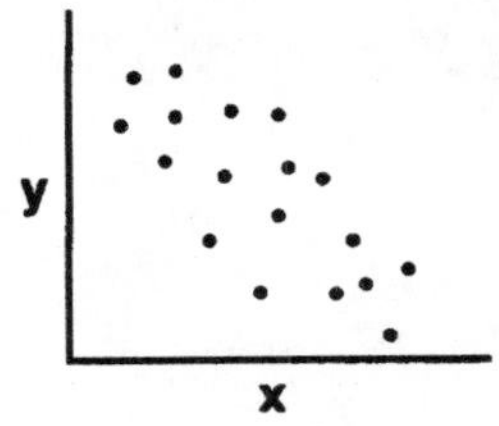

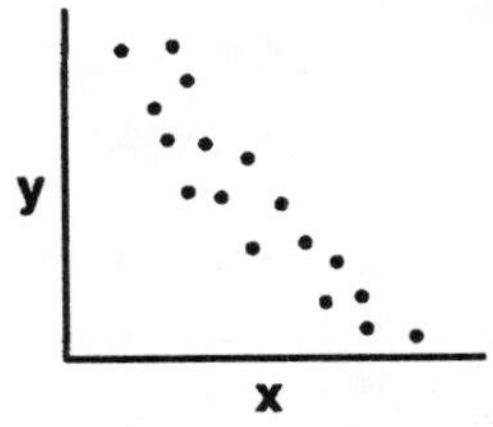

Figure 5-11 *These five scatter diagrams show various possible correlations between the two variables, from positive to negative.*

Source: GOAL/QPC: *The Memory Jogger: A Pocket Guide of Tools for Continuous Improvement.* Methuen, MA: GOAL/QPC, 1988. Used with permission.

Benefits

Although they may not conclusively prove a relationship between two variables, scatter diagrams can offer persuasive evidence. They help a team confirm or abandon its suspicion that one variable is linked to another. Teams can use scatter diagrams to gauge the relative strength of their theories and to monitor the effects of their actions.

Examples

- The scatter diagram shown in Figure 5-10 tests the relationship between patient waiting time and hospital occupancy. The findings show a strong positive correlation between these two variables.
- A few other possible sets of variables whose relationship might be tested using a scatter diagram include
  - patient outcome for a given procedure and number of procedures performed;
  - patient satisfaction and number of staff on a given unit;
  - patient outcome and time spent on patient education; and
  - medication cost per case and total cost per case.

REVIEW OF PROCEDURE

1. Decide which two variables will be tested.
2. Collect and record relevant data.
3. Draw the horizontal and vertical axes.
4. Plot the variables on the graph.
5. Interpret the completed diagram.

References

1. GOAL/QPC: *The Memory Jogger*. Methuen, MA: GOAL/QPC, 1988, pp 57–58.
2. GOAL/QPC: *The Memory Jogger*. Methuen, MA: GOAL/QPC, 1988, p. 39
3. GOAL/QPC: *The Memory Jogger*. Methuen, MA: GOAL/QPC, 1988, p. 46.

Section 6

Tools for Understanding Root Causes of Performance

An important facet of data analysis is finding root causes of performance. That information can help determine characteristics of strong and efficient processes, which may be applied to other processes in an organization. Information about root causes of performance also can help a team determine specific changes necessary to improve a process. The tools in this section are designed to help understand processes and understand factors that contribute to both good and problematic performance.

Flowcharts help groups understand the steps in a current process and design improved processes. Cause-and-effect diagrams help groups gather a list of reasons a specific outcome or effect may occur. Pareto charts illustrate which causes of a particular outcome are most frequent and, therefore, worthy of attention.

The tools in this section are among the most popular and persuasive of performance improvement. None of these tools requires a statistical background (although Pareto charts are quantitative tools).

Flowcharts

A flowchart is a graphic representation of the path a process follows from start to finish. Flowcharts are designed to help teams understand all steps in a process through the use of common, easily recognizable symbols. Clear understanding of process is essential if improvement is to take place. Flowcharts can illustrate the *actual* path a process takes or the *ideal* path a process should follow.

Flowcharts are widely used to identify problems and plan solutions. They should be used whenever a team needs to identify the path that a product or service follows in order to spot problem areas and opportunities for improvement.

Process

Creating a flowchart may be a time-consuming endeavor. Keep in mind that difficulties likely reflect confusion in the process being charted, and work through them. The following steps should help move a team toward creating a successful flowchart:

1. **Define the process to be flowcharted.** This step helps contain the chart within manageable boundaries. One of the most common problems teams encounter in trying to create flowcharts is that they find themselves examining a system rather than a process within a system. Once team members begin to create a flowchart, if they find themselves with a process that seems prohibitively confusing, they should create a simple high-level flowchart containing only the most basic components. Such a chart may help a team see that it is tackling a system rather than a process and also help identify the process that needs to be addressed. Once a process is chosen, specific boundaries of that process should be identified.

2. **Brainstorm activities and decision points in the process.** Look for specific activities and decisions necessary to keep the process moving to its conclusion. This should be done by those most familiar with the various parts of the process, with assistance as necessary from people outside the team. One pitfall that teams encounter at this stage is trying to include too much detail in the analysis; be wary of obscuring the basic process with too many minor components.

3. **Determine the sequence of activities and decision points.** Some activities may appear to occur simultaneously, while others may seem disconnected; certain decisions may cause steps to be repeated. Initially, teams can use adhesive notes placed on a wall to experiment with sequence until the appropriate one is determined.

4. **Use this information to create the flowchart.** Place each activity in a box and place each decision point in a diamond. Connect these with lines and arrows to indicate the flow of the process. (See Figure 6-1, page 101, for common flowchart symbols and Figure 6-2, page 102, for a generic flowchart.)

5. **Analyze the flowchart.** Look for redundancies, black holes, barriers, and any other difficulties. Make sure that every feedback loop has an escape. Make the chart the basis for designing an improved process, using spots where the process works well as models for improvement. The team may want to create a separate flowchart that represents the ideal path of the process, and then compare the two charts for discrepancies.

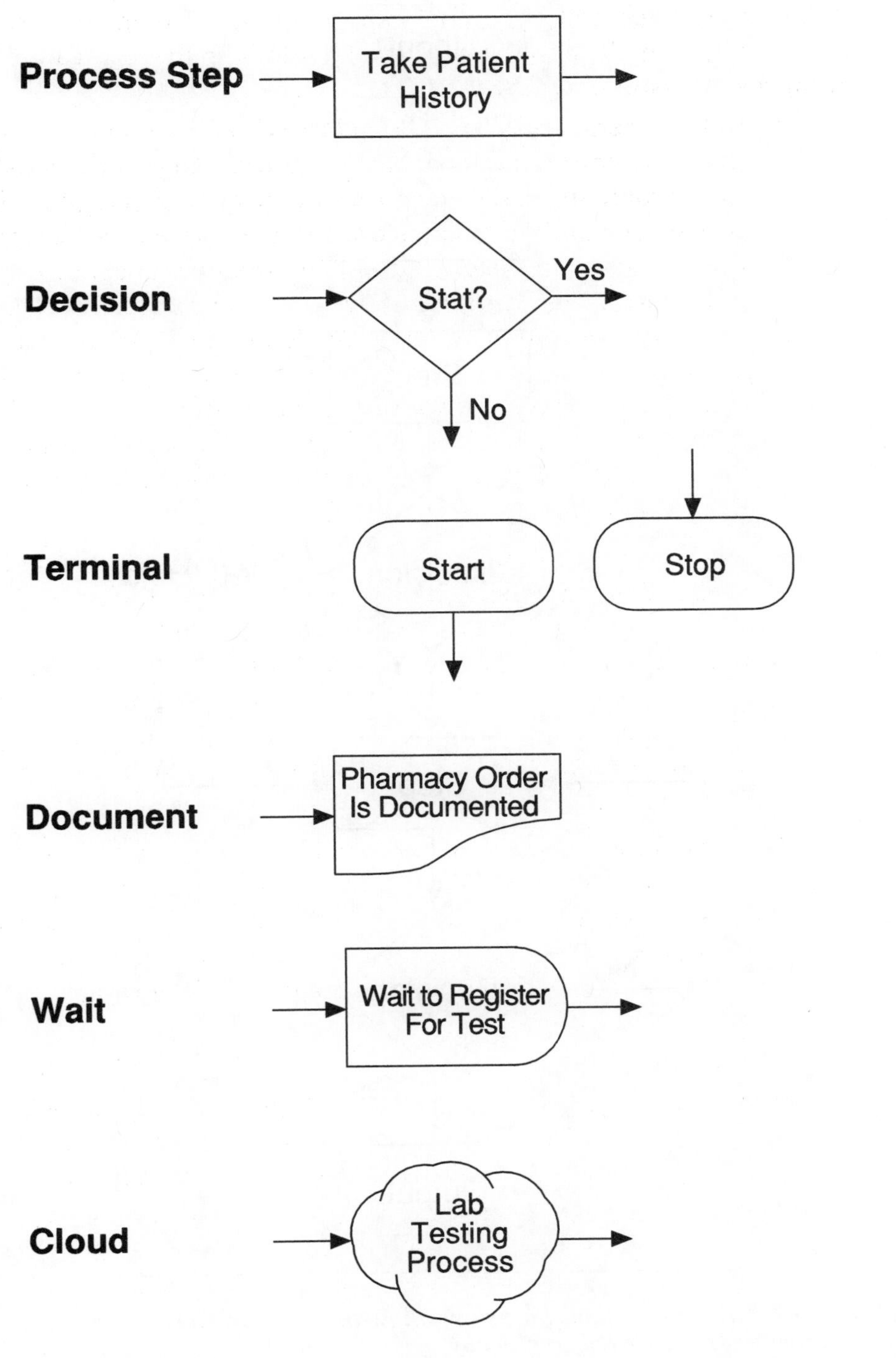

Figure 6-1 *These symbols are used to illustrate various parts of a process in a flowchart.*

Generic Flowchart

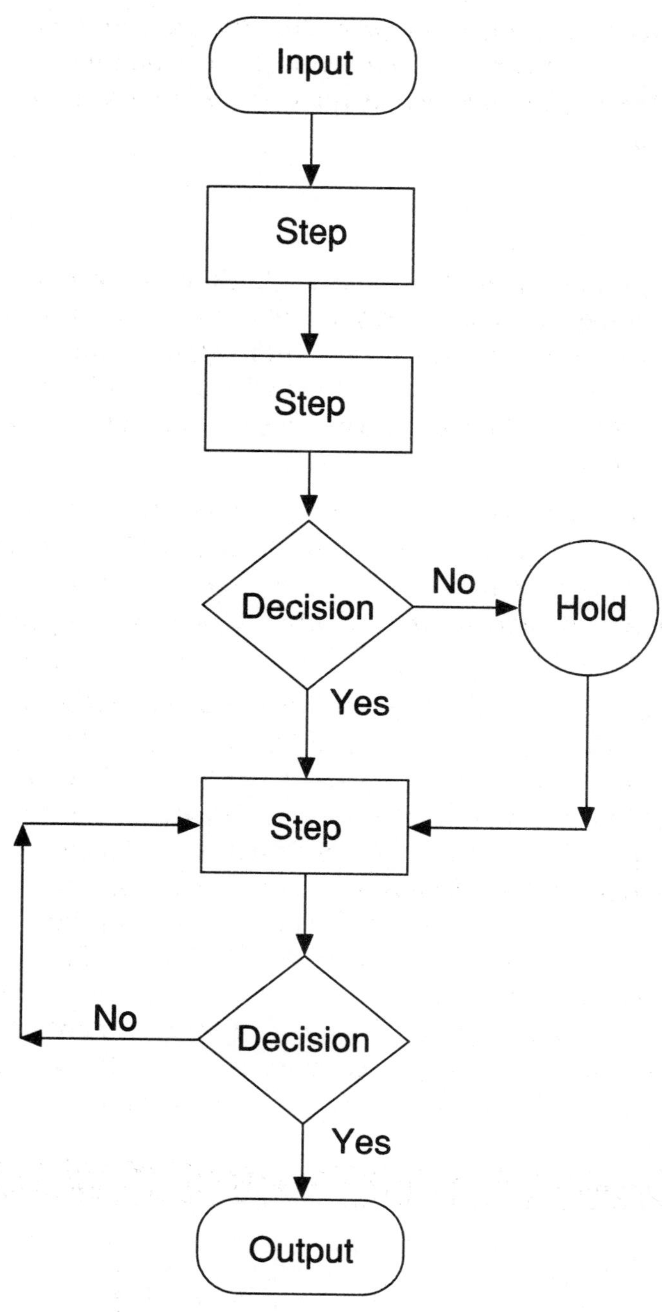

Figure 6-2 *This generic flowchart shows how the components of a process and their sequence are displayed graphically.*

Benefits

Flowcharts help identify inefficiencies, misunderstandings, redundancies, and areas of neglect, while providing insight into how a given process should be performed. They show a clear picture of the process and provide the people involved at the various steps with an understanding of the whole.

Examples

- Figure 6-3 (page 104) shows a high-level flowchart of a system, which encompasses various processes. The example identifies key steps of the outpatient billing system and illustrates the sequence of those steps along with a few substeps. Such a flowchart can help a team visualize the big picture of a system or process.
- Figure 6-4 (page 105) shows a more detailed flowchart. This chart shows the inputs, outputs, and decision points in the process by which patients make their way through the emergency department. In addition, the chart lists several barriers to patient flow.
- Figure 6-5 (page 106) shows a unique approach to flowcharting. This chart, called an "instrument panel" by its creators, shows two processes related to access: the appointment process and the process for responding to patient phone calls. Each step of these processes is phrased as a measurable indicator. Underneath each step is shown the findings of data collected for that indicator. For example, one step in the appointment process is "time in exam room." Beneath that step is listed the percentage of patients, within one year, who waited less than ten minutes and who waited more than ten minutes in each of three clinics. This format helps viewers see the relationship between the process and actual performance.

REVIEW OF PROCEDURE

1. Define the process to be flowcharted.
2. Brainstorm activities and decision points in the process.
3. Determine the sequence of activities and decision points.
4. Use this information to create the flowchart.
5. Analyze the flowchart.

High-Level Flowchart: Outpatient Billing

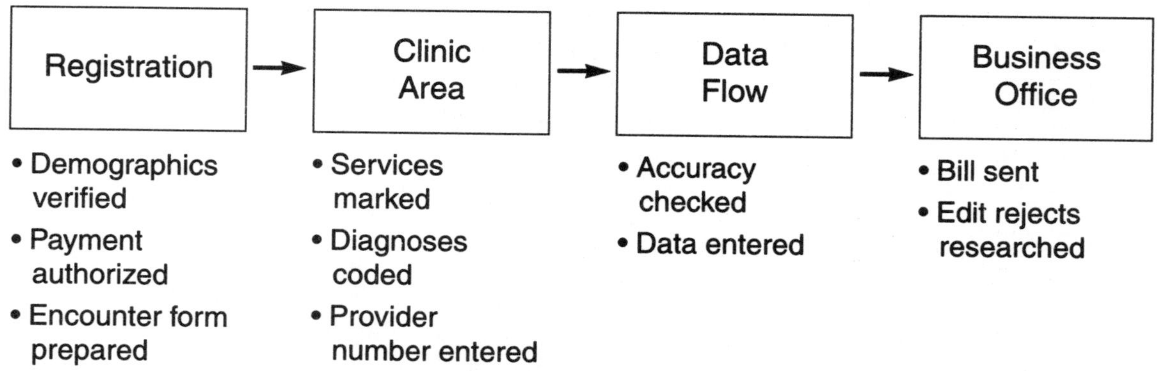

Registration →	Clinic Area →	Data Flow →	Business Office
• Demographics verified • Payment authorized • Encounter form prepared	• Services marked • Diagnoses coded • Provider number entered	• Accuracy checked • Data entered	• Bill sent • Edit rejects researched

Figure 6-3 *This high-level flowchart is a simplified view of the components in a broad system.*

Cause-and-Effect Diagrams

Also called Ishikawa diagrams or *fishbone diagrams* (because of their shape), cause-and-effect diagrams are helpful in the improvement process because they present a clear picture of the many causal relationships between outcomes and factors in those outcomes. These diagrams are designed to identify and display large numbers of possible causes for each outcome or problem that a team targets for improvement (such as equipment failures or medication errors).

Cause-and-effect diagrams are used to identify problems or specific parts of a process to target for improvement. They may also be used any time a team wants to know why specific problems or conditions occur. When used in connection with other tools, they are also helpful in data analysis.

Process

Creating a cause-and-effect diagram may proceed quickly or may take considerable time. The key is to identify as many causes as possible. Team members' experience and expertise are the most valuable resources for adding content to a cause-and-effect diagram.

The following steps outline the process for creating a cause-and-effect diagram:

1. **Identify the outcome or problem statement.** This statement defines the effect for which the team will identify possible causes. Place the outcome on the right side of the page, halfway down, and then draw an arrow horizontally across the page, pointing to the outcome. The arrow will focus attention on the outcome and provide the main axis of the diagram.

Flowchart: Emergency Department (ED) Patient Flow

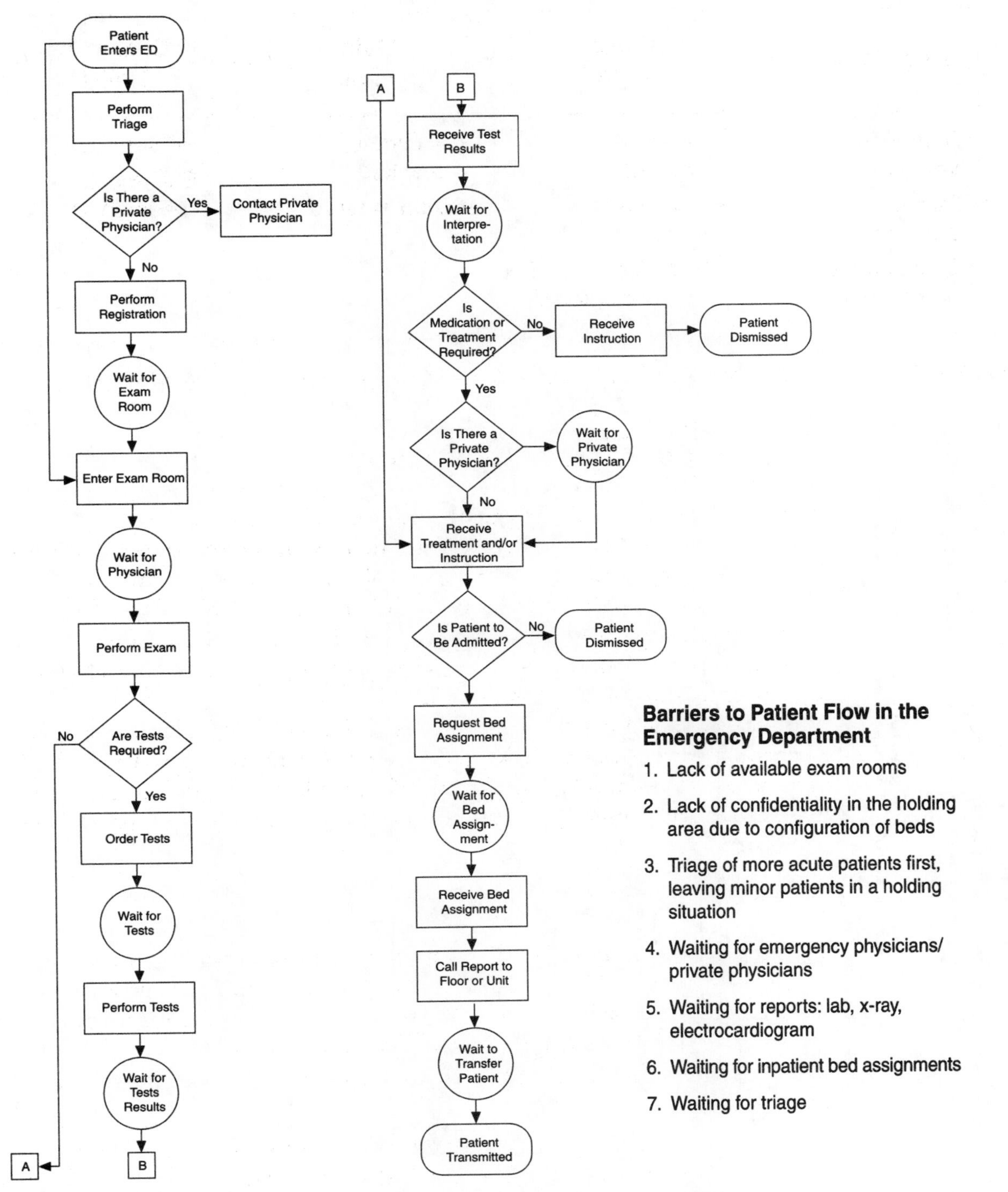

Figure 6-4 *This flowchart illustrates the complex process of patient flow through an emergency department. Accompanying the chart are several barriers noted by the team studying the process.*
Source: Integris Baptist Medical Center, Oklahoma City. Used with permission.

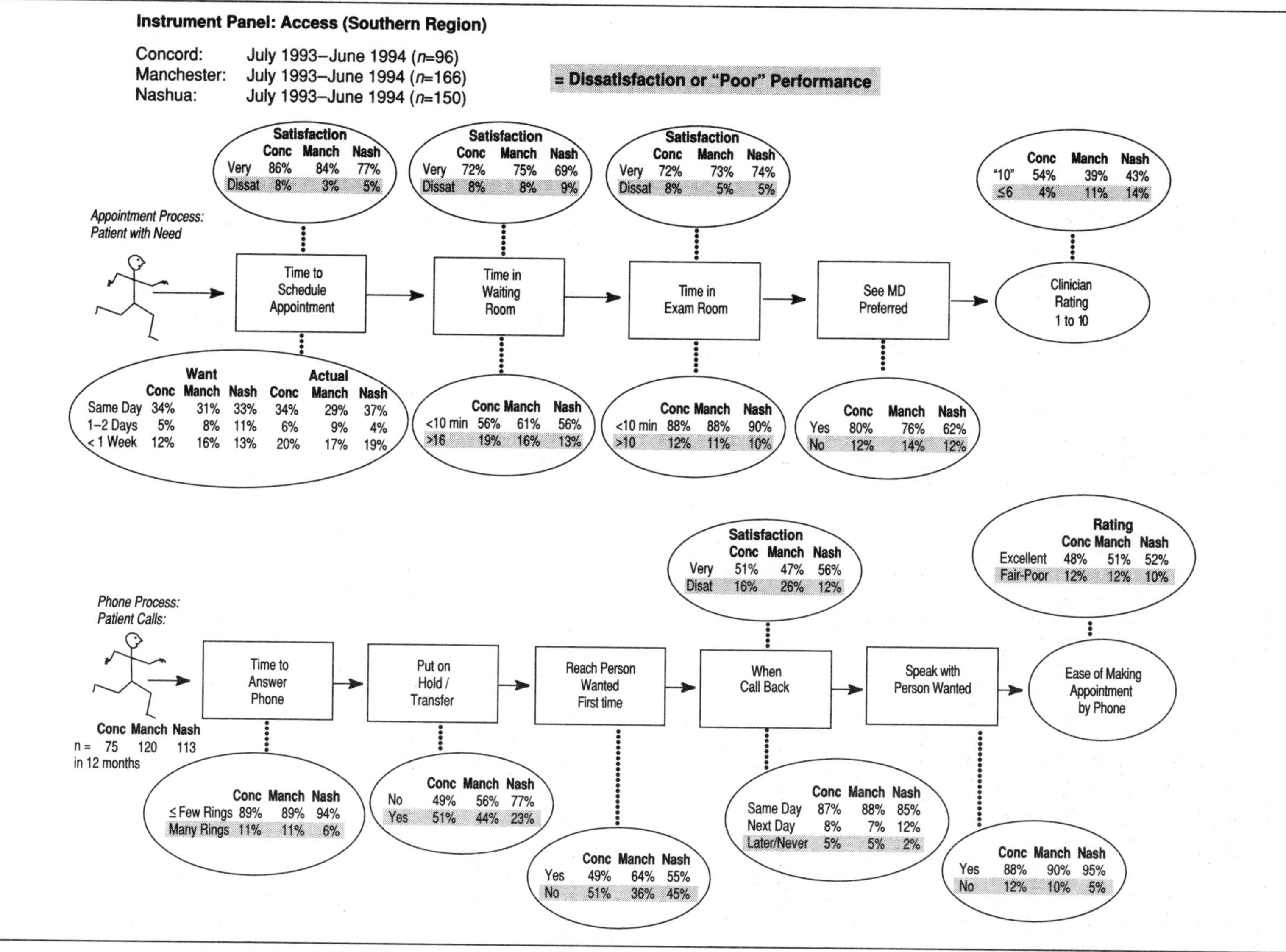

Figure 6-5 *This figure shows a tool that melds flowcharting and data display. The chart illustrates the basic steps in two processes related to patient access—the appointment process and the process for handling patient calls. For each step, performance findings are shown for three regions in this health care system.*

Source: Nelson EC et al: Report cards or instrument panels: Who needs what? *Jt Comm J Qual Immov* 21(4): 162, 1995. The Lahey Hitchcock Clinic, Bedford, NH. Used with permission.

2. **Determine general categories for the causes.** Common categories include work methods, personnel, materials, and equipment. Represent these on the diagram by connecting them with diagonal lines branching off from the main horizontal line. (A generic cause-and-effect diagram is shown in Figure 6-6, below.)

3. **List major causes under the general categories.** Brainstorm to come up with major causes. They should be more specific than the general categories but may still have more specific subcauses. Team members should ask *why* or *how* at least five times. Place each main cause on a horizontal line connected to the appropriate diagonal line.

4. **List subcauses and place them under the major causes.** Not every major cause will have a subcause, but try to find any relevant causes that contribute to the major causes. Use smaller diagonal lines to connect them to the major causes.

5. **Evaluate the diagram.** When all ideas have been noted, the team should study the diagram to determine obvious areas for improvement, causes that are readily solved or eliminated, and areas needing study so that they can be better understood.

Benefits

The diagram's appearance helps team members and others quickly visualize how various components relate to one another. Cause-and-effect diagrams lead teams to conclusions about specific causes and help the team develop solutions to problems.

Generic Cause-and-Effect Diagram

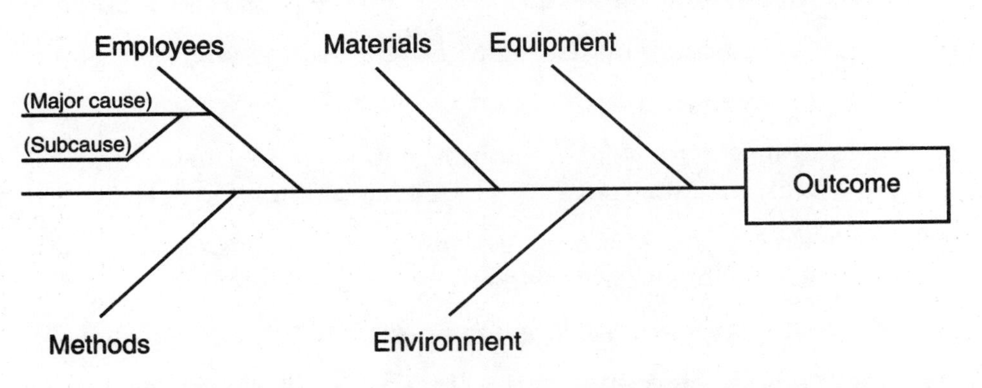

Figure 6-6 *This figure shows the basic features of a cause-and-effect diagram: a central axis pointing toward an outcome with major causes and subcauses—separated into groups—that potentially lead to that outcome.*

REVIEW OF PROCEDURE

1. Identify the outcome or problem statement.
2. Determine general categories for the causes.
3. List major causes under the general categories.
4. List subcauses and place them under the major causes.
5. Evaluate the diagram.

Examples

- Figure 6-7 (page 109) shows how a cause-and-effect diagram was used to document factors contributing to long response times for a hospital patient and specimen transportation department.Note that the causes are divided into the following major categories: people, measurements, materials/inputs, method, and machines.
- Figure 6-8 (page 110) lists the factors that contribute to the decision to perform a repeat cesarean section(C-section). In this example, the causes are divided into groups labeled mother, baby, and physician. Such a chart can help a team studying this issue decide which factor to address in its improvement actions. A Pareto chart would be an ideal tool for measuring and analyzing which factor most often contributes to the decision to perform a repeat C-section. Such a chart is found in Figure 6-9 (page 111) along with the description of Pareto charts.

TIPS FOR CREATING AND INTERPRETING CAUSE-AND-EFFECT DIAGRAMS

- Make sure everyone agrees completely on the problem statement.
- Minimize frustration by staying within the group's realm of control.
- Use as few words as possible.
- Keep asking *why* to avoid the common mistake of thinking the team has arrived at a root cause long before it actually has.
- If the team gets stuck, use the general categories as catalysts; ask what in each category is causing the particular outcome.
- In the evaluation process, look for causes that appear repeatedly.
- Gather data to determine relative frequencies of the causes.
- Focus more on system causes than on causes associated with individual performance.

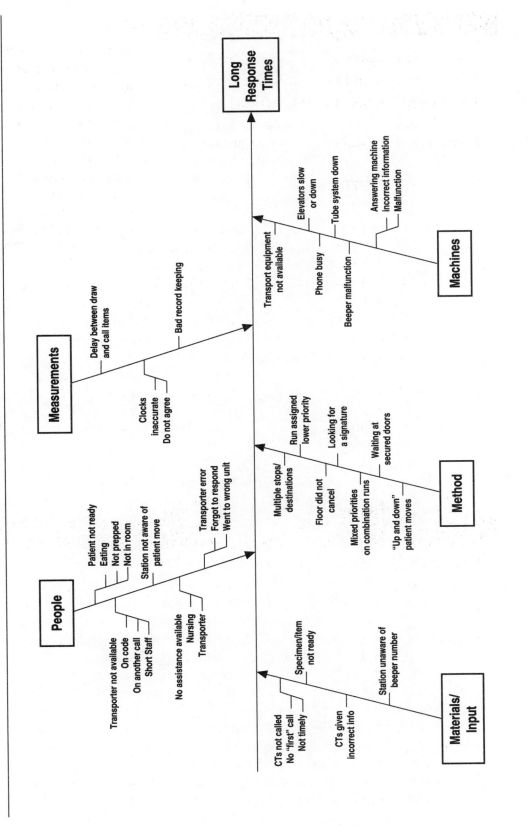

Figure 6-7 *This cause-and-effect diagram groups and displays the significant causes and subcauses of long response times for hospital patient and specimen transportation.*

Source: Maricopa Medical Center, Phoenix, AZ. Used with permission.

Cause-and-Effect Diagram:
Decision to Perform Repeat Cesarean Section (C-Section)

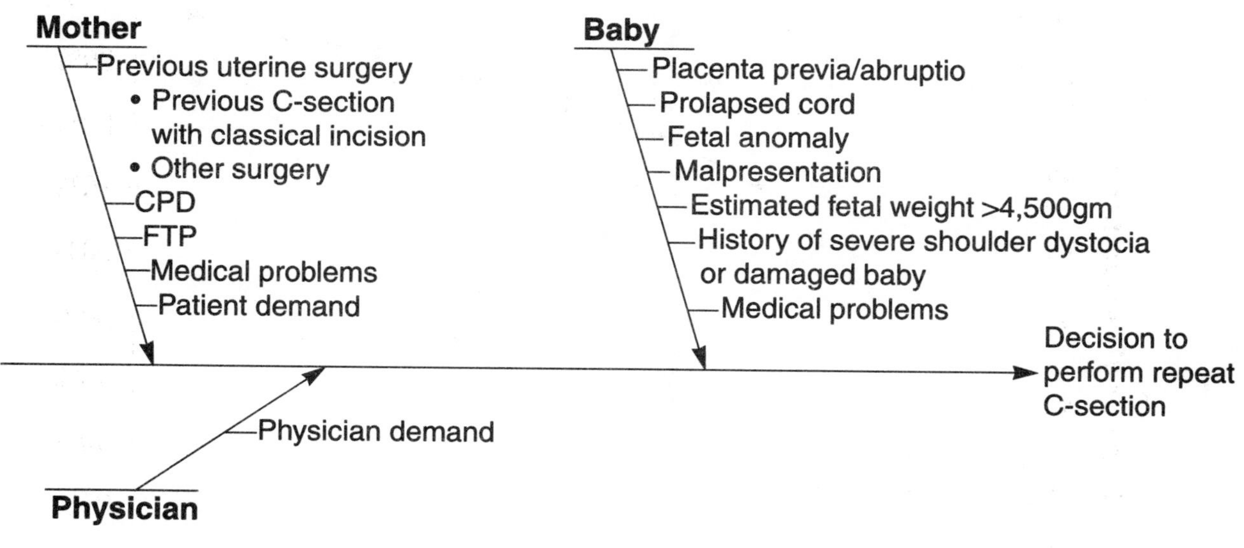

Figure 6-8 *In this example, a cause-and-effect diagram helps trace the circumstances leading to a clinical decision.*

Source: Used with permission from *Reengineering Health Care: Building on CQI* by John R. Griffith, et al (Chicago: Health Administration Press, 1995), p 234.

- A cause-and-effect diagram can identify causes of desirable, as well as undesirable, outcomes, such as high retention rates. Causes of high retention rates might include staff recognition, good benefits, and career opportunities, among others.

Pareto Charts

The Pareto principle holds that a few causes are responsible for the majority of effects. A Pareto chart is a type of statistical tool used to compare events, problems, or causes according to their relative frequency or magnitude. The chart uses a vertical bar graph format to show this comparison, with elements arranged in descending order from left to right. The purpose of the Pareto chart is to show teams which events or causes have the greatest effects and therefore help determine which problems to solve in what order.

Pareto charts are used to determine the relative importance of a number of conditions in order to choose the starting point for problem solving. They also are used to evaluate the success of team efforts. A Pareto chart is a natural follow-up to a cause-and-effect diagram and can easily be constructed from data collected on a check sheet.

Pareto Chart: Causes of Repeat Cesarean Sections

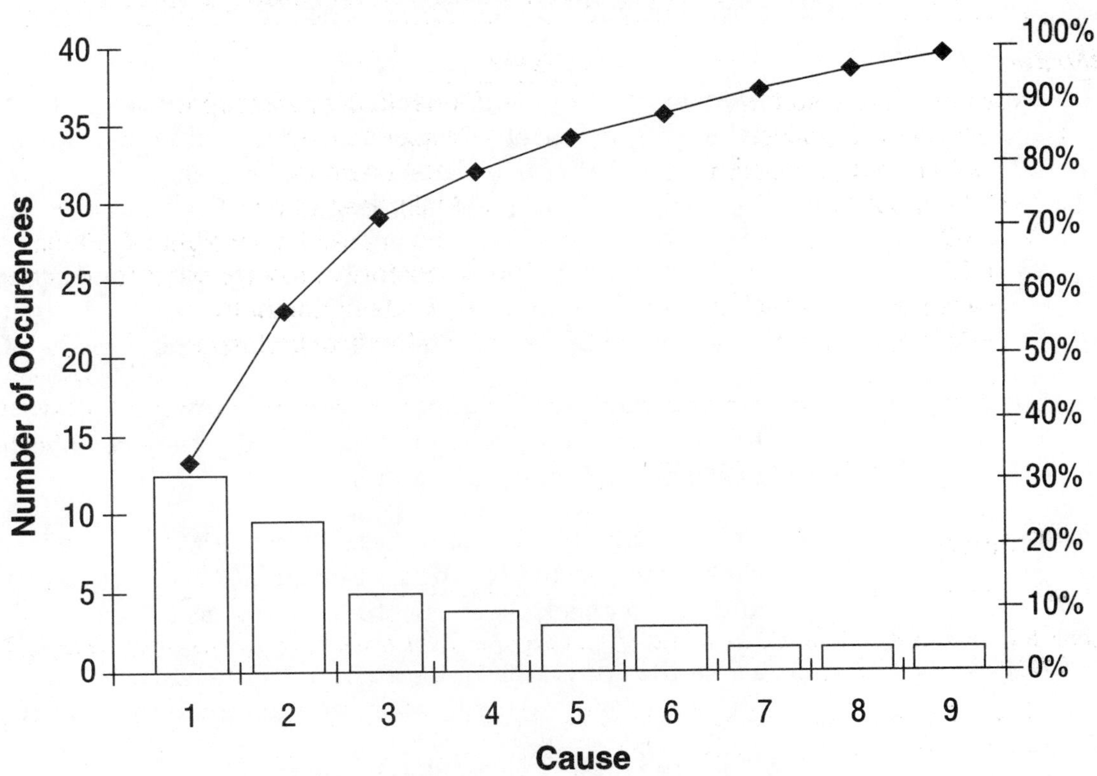

Label	Cause	Value	%	Cum. %
1	Cardiopulmonary distress/ failure to progress	12	32	32
2	Patient request	10	27	59
3	Fetal distress	5	14	73
4	Breech	3	8	81
5	Fetal medical problems	2	5	86
6	Maternal medical problems	2	5	91
7	Previous uterine surgery	1	3	94
8	Placenta previa/abruptio	1	3	97
9	Fetal anomaly	1	35	100

Figure 6-9 *This example shows how a Pareto chart can be a logical follow-up to a cause-and-effect diagram. In this case, the cause-and-effect diagram in Figure 6-8 shows potential causes for the decision to perform a repeat cesarean section. This Pareto chart displays the results of data collection done to determine the relative frequency of these causes. As most Pareto charts show, a few causes are responsible for the majority of occurrences.*

Source: Used with permission from *Reengineering Health Care: Building on CQI* by John R. Griffith, et al (Chicago: Health Administration Press, 1995), p 235.

Process

The following steps guide a team to successful creation and use of a Pareto chart:

1. **Decide on a topic of study.** The topic can be any outcome for which a number of potential causes has been identified. If the team is working from a cause-and-effect diagram, the topic will be the effect that the team has targeted for improvement.

2. **Select causes or conditions to be compared.** Identify the factors that contribute to the outcome—the more specific the better. This is where the cause-and-effect diagram is particularly helpful.

3. **Set the standard for comparison.** In many cases, the standard for comparison is frequency. Factors also may be compared based on their cost or quantity.

4. **Collect data.** If this is not already done, determine how often each factor occurs (or the cost or quantity of each, as appropriate). Use a check sheet to help with this task.

5. **Make the comparison.** Based on the data collected in the previous step, compare the factors and rank them from most to least.

6. **Draw the chart's vertical axis.** On the left side of the chart, draw a vertical line and mark the standard of measurement in increments.

7. **List factors along the horizontal axis.** Place the name of each factor across the bottom of the chart. Factors should be arranged in descending order, with the highest-ranking factor at the far left.

8. **Draw a bar for each factor.** The bars represent how often each factor occurs, the cost of each factor, or its quantity, as applicable.

9. **Include additional features if desired.** By making a few simple additions to the Pareto chart, a team can show the cumulative frequency, cost, or quantity of the categories in percentages. To do this, add a vertical percentage scale to the right side of the chart, where 100% is opposite the total frequency shown on the left and 50% is opposite the halfway point in the raw data. Be sure these are drawn to scale. Next, add a line that moves upward from left to right to represent how far toward the cumulative total each factor reaches. This can help the team see when the causes comprise the majority of outcomes.

Benefits

Through the comparison of specific factors, Pareto charts help teams focus their attention on those areas that are the most promising targets for improvement. By creating subsequent Pareto charts using the original factors, a team also can do "before and after" comparisons to measure its effect as it moves through the improvement process.

Examples

- Figure 6-9 shows a Pareto chart that corresponds to the cause-and-effect chart for repeat C-sections in Figure 6-8. The Pareto chart displays the relative frequency for the causes identified as leading to repeat C-sections. The two most frequent of the causes (cardiopulmonary distress/failure to progress and patient request) account for 59% of decisions to perform a repeat C-section. Adding the third cause, fetal distress, brings the total to 73%.
- The Pareto chart in Figure 6-10 (page 114) shows the relative frequency of medication errors in different patient care areas. This finding helps a team focus its attention on activities that will have the strongest effect on reducing the medication error rate.
- In Figure 6-11 (page 115) a Pareto chart displays how often various causes lead to cancellation of outpatient surgery. As in the previous example, the chart's findings can focus a team's attention—in this case, on a portion of the process for outpatient surgery preparation.

REVIEW OF PROCEDURE

1. Decide on a topic of study.
2. Select causes or conditions to be compared.
3. Set the standard for comparison.
4. Collect data.
5. Make the comparison.
6. Draw the chart's vertical axis.
7. List factors along the horizontal axis.
8. Draw a bar for each factor.
9. Include additional features if desired.

TIPS FOR CONSTRUCTION AND INTERPRETATION

- When selecting factors for comparison, beware of grouping several distinct problems together, which can skew the rank order. Refer to the cause-and-effect diagram, and use the most specific causes and factors possible.
- Be sure to mark the chart clearly to show the standard of measurement. Do the numbers represent frequency, dollar amounts, quantity, or percentages?
- When analyzing your chart, keep in mind that numbers do not always tell the whole story. Sometimes 2 severe complaints deserve more attention than 100 other complaints.

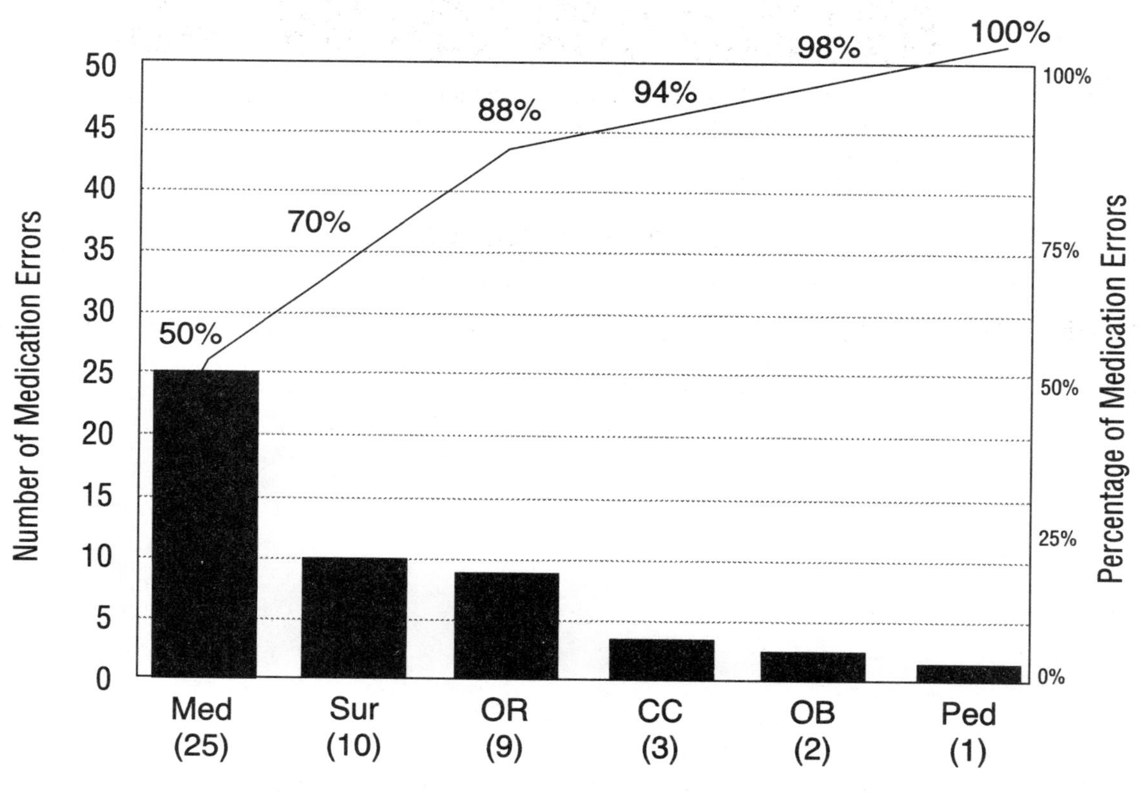

Figure 6-10 *This Pareto chart shows the relative frequency of medication errors according to their location.*

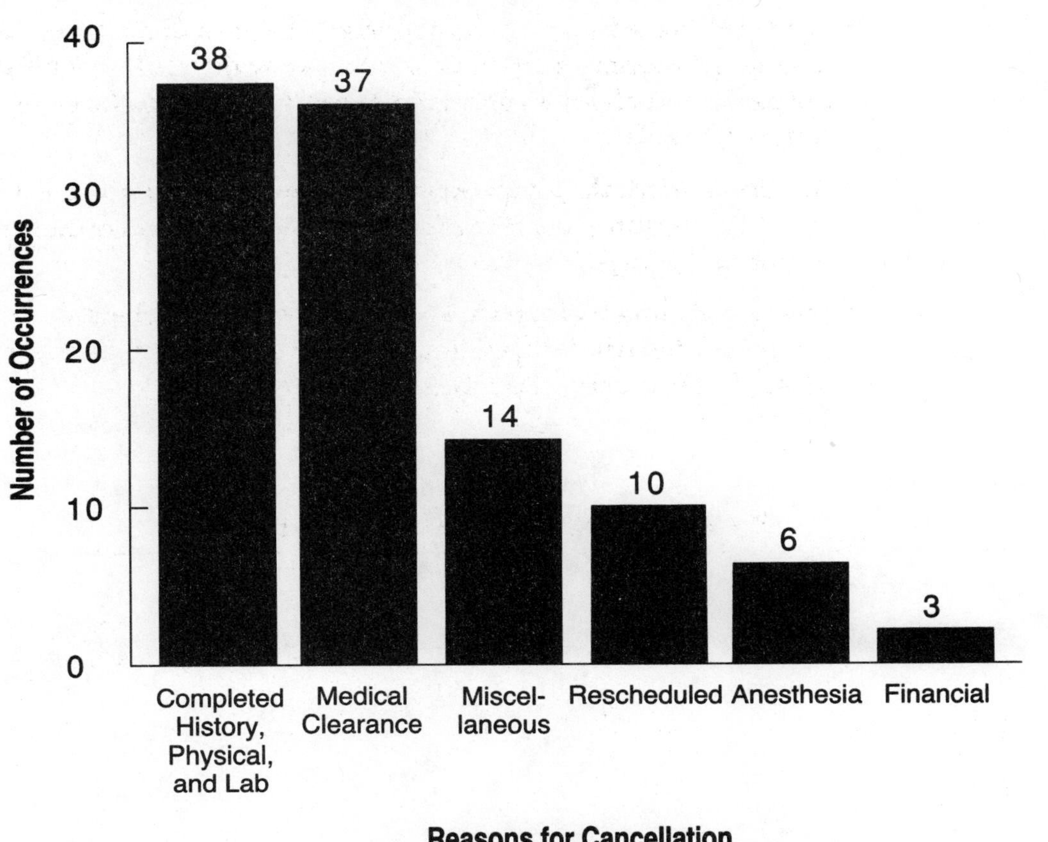

Figure 6-11 *This Pareto chart ranks the frequency of various causes of outpatient surgery cancellation.*

Section 7 Case Studies

The case studies in this section show how two health care organizations used some of the tools described in this book as part of a systematic effort to improve an aspect of care. These cases have been chosen to help readers understand not just the isolated purpose of each tool, but how those tools can function together and can help an improvement team in a real-world situation.

These examples are as notable for what they do not show as for what they do show. They do not show subjective analysis, directionless teams, blame on individuals, turf battles, and actions that address only surface causes. They *do* show effective teamwork, specific purposes, focus on processes rather than on individuals, objective analysis, and actions directed at root causes.

The presentation of these examples is purposely simplified, showing the basic steps, the use of tools, the opportunities for improvement, and the actions taken. Readers should get an overview of how the process as a whole functions and how some of the tools discussed in the previous chapters work in practice.

The Patient-Transfer Project

Bellin Health Systems is a 180-bed community medical center, 87-bed freestanding psychiatric hospital, and college of nursing in Green Bay, Wisconsin. One of the hospital's early performance improvement projects focused on the process for transferring patients to 2-South—the medical cardiac floor—from intensive care units. For some time, this process was subject to difficulties that were problematic for both patients and staff. The performance improvement project involved forming a multidisciplinary team that brought together people who had previously often found themselves in adversarial positions. The team worked together to understand the patient-transfer process, assess current performance of the process, find root causes based on that assessment, implement actions aimed at these root causes, monitor the effectiveness of these actions, and make further changes as necessary.

Performance Improvement Techniques

This improvement team primarily used flowcharts, histograms, cause-and-effect diagrams, brainstorming, and run charts. The flowcharts helped the team document the current patient-transfer process and to design an improved process. The histograms were used to understand the distribution of transfer times and to see how corrective actions changed that distribution. A cause-and-effect diagram helped the team uncover many potential causes for the patient-transfer problems; brainstorming helped the team come up with these causes. A run chart monitored overall performance after process changes were implemented.

Team members were taught about the quality improvement tools as a group as the team was in progress. Training was done by the quality education manager, who was the team's facilitator. The quality education manager and the team leader (a charge nurse) were primarily responsible for choosing the appropriate tools.

Were the tools helpful? "Definitely," says Jeff Matzke, registered nurse educator, who was a member of the team. "They gave a clear picture of where we were and where we needed to go; they were really visual and helped us see the improvements as we went along."

Matzke adds that in other groups he has found Pareto charts to be easy-to-use and helpful tools. He says that control charts are now being more widely used in the hospital. The growing use of such tools is, he reports, due to hospitalwide quality improvement training. "With that knowledge, we're getting more comfortable with the QI process."

But what about the statistical skills necessary for control charts? "When the reports come out and you see the diagrams, people have no problem with that; [however,] there can be trouble with the creation of the control chart." To overcome this difficulty, Bellin has computer programs that use raw data to create control charts and show standard deviations from a mean. In addition, says Matzke, at Bellin "we do have a number of core people who have training in statistics."

On a more general note, Matzke suggests that team members must be aware of the amount of time involved in the quality improvement process. "They want to get in and get it done and move on," he says. "The biggest hurdle is just to explain that it will take time to get in and find the root causes of the problems and that this process is a little slower than what they are used to." Matzke also stresses the importance of meeting attendance. If teams are to be successful, Matzke says, "you need to make sure everyone gets there on a regular basis."

The following sections trace the activities of this team.

Process Used

At Bellin, quality improvement teams use a process called VALUE PLUS+ to assess and improve care and service. The steps are as follows:

- Verify that a problem exists;
- Assemble a team;
- Locate and isolate the problem;
- Uncover potential theories;
- Establish the real causes of the problem;
- Plan for the remedy of the problem;
- Learn by testing the remedy;
- Understand the impact of implementing the remedy;
- Solidify the change; and
- + Recognize and celebrate.

Verify That a Problem Exists

Within Bellin Hospital, patient transfer from the critical care unit (CCU) and the intermediate care unit (IMCU) to 2-South was a nagging problem. Units blamed and struggled with one another, resulting in transfers occurring at inappropriate times of the day. In turn, this inappropriateness caused staffing difficulties, patient backlogs, transfer delays, staff frustration, stress, overtime, and patient anxiety.

To end the struggle, the hospital began by establishing a one-sentence problem statement describing the current difficulties. Then it developed this mission statement: "To develop a process to facilitate timely and efficient patient transfers."

Assemble a Team

To carry out this improvement mission, Bellin initially assembled a team composed of charge and staff nurses from each area. The quality education manager served as facilitator. Later, the team realized it needed other forms of expertise besides nursing to address this process. The environmental services manager and transportation manager were added as consultants, and patient/family input was also important.

The unit managers were not on the team, but they supported the team and approved the team's proposed actions. Bellin reports that "the managers' absence from team meetings, yet ever-present support, led team members on a journey that started with blame and ended with mutual trust and respect for the people involved in the process."

The team's initial challenge was to learn to trust one another after a considerable period of distrust. During initial meetings, the philosophy of process versus people was stressed: improvement results from changing bad processes, not from blaming individuals. The team still was not mutually trusting early in the process; only when it got to the "uncover potential theories" stage did it realize that processes, not people, were at the problem's root.

Locate and Isolate the Problem

To describe the current process, the team created the flowchart shown in Figure 7-1 (page 121). The team hoped that this chart would show areas in which delays occurred. In Figure 7-1 those areas are enclosed in the large box. Difficulties arose when transfers were not urgent. For these nonurgent transfers, a series of delays and negotiations would take place.

The team also organized data to determine at what time of day transfers took place. (Timing was an issue the team tentatively believed was one root cause of delay, as reflected in the problem statement.) The histogram in Figure 7-2 (page 122) shows these data, whose distribution is not normal. There were three peak transfer times: 9 AM to 12:30 PM, 1 PM to 5:30 PM, and 7 PM. In other words, the time range for transfer was not predictable.

Uncover Potential Theories

Next, the team attempted to understand why the delays and the unpredictable timing took place. To learn more about the causes, the team developed a cause-and-effect diagram. The causes were grouped into five general categories: space, staff, methods, time, and materials. The team used the brainstorming technique to come up with specific causes under these general categories. Key causes were variation in number of transfers, lack of nurses, time of transfer, and lack of bed or private rooms. Figure 7-3 (page 123) shows this cause-and-effect diagram.

Establish the Real Causes of the Problem

The team analyzed the causes it listed to find common factors. Ultimately, the members found that unpredictability of transfers was at the root of many of the other causes: lack of beds or private rooms; lack of nurses; housekeeping staff unavailable; wheelchairs/carts unavailable; variations

Flowchart: Patient Transfer from CCU/IMCU to 2-South

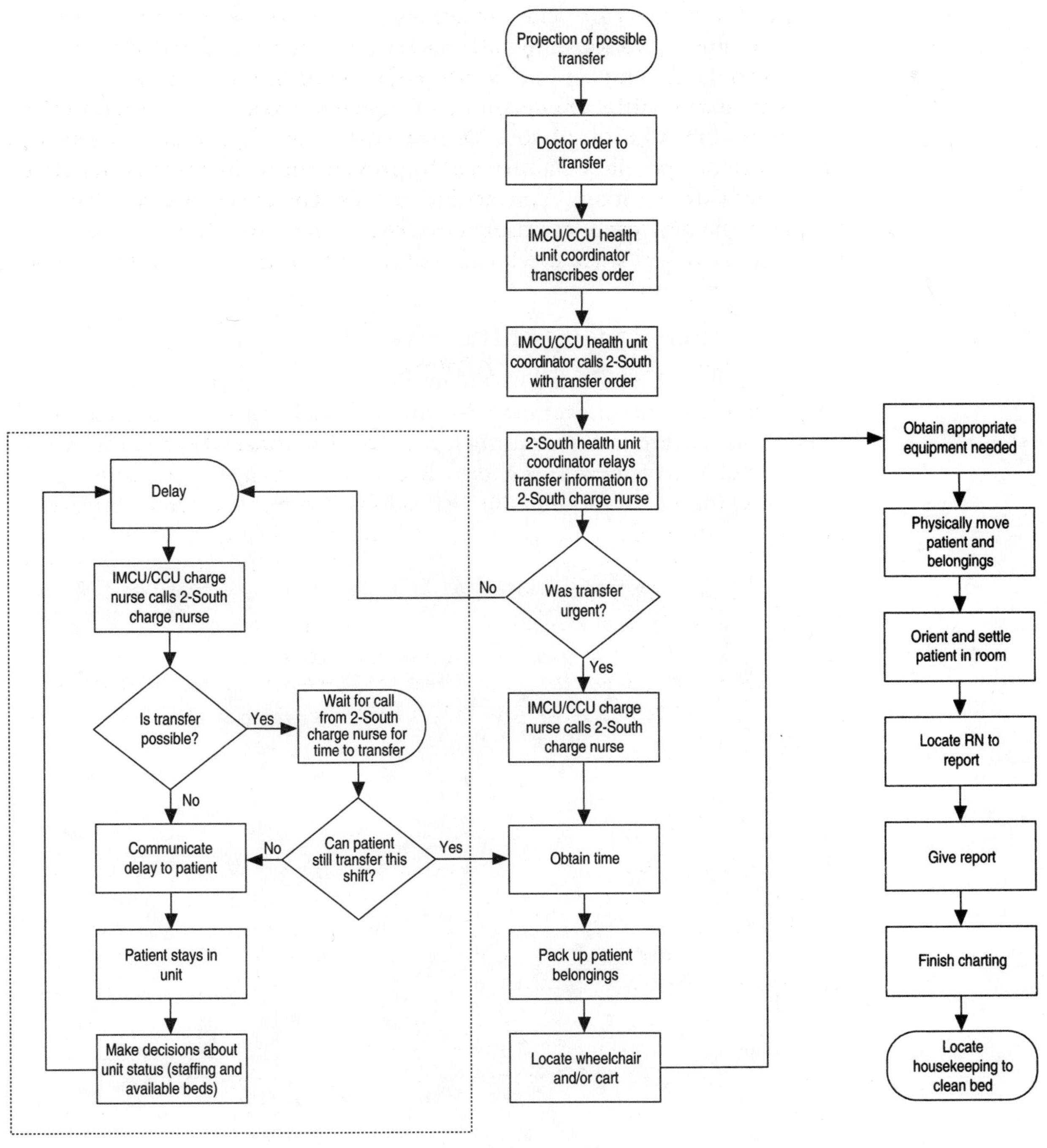

Figure 7-1 *This chart illustrates the patient-transfer process as it was first analyzed by the improvement team. The area of difficulty is enclosed within the dashed-line box.*

Source: Bellin Health Systems, Green Bay, WI. Used with permission.

in number of transfers; communication breakdown; inappropriate time of transfer, such as during shift changes; time order obtained; time bed is available; and time for receiving nurses to get report.

Therefore, the team's hypothesis was that if transfers could be predicted the day before they occurred, staff would be prepared to accommodate and accept the predicted number of transfers in a timely manner, thus alleviating change-of-shift transfers and many of the other issues.

The team developed a formula for predicting next-day transfers based on historical data. Also, based on experience and data, the team specified the best times for transfers as 9:30 AM to 10:30 AM and 1 PM to 2:30 PM.

Plan for the Remedy of the Problem

Based on the data collected, the team developed a new transfer process, instituting the newly developed formula to predict next-day transfers, which was used to adjust staffing levels, and the newly specified transfer times, which were used to schedule transfers.

The process was significantly simplified from the previous one. In

Histogram: CCU/IMCU Transfers to 2-South

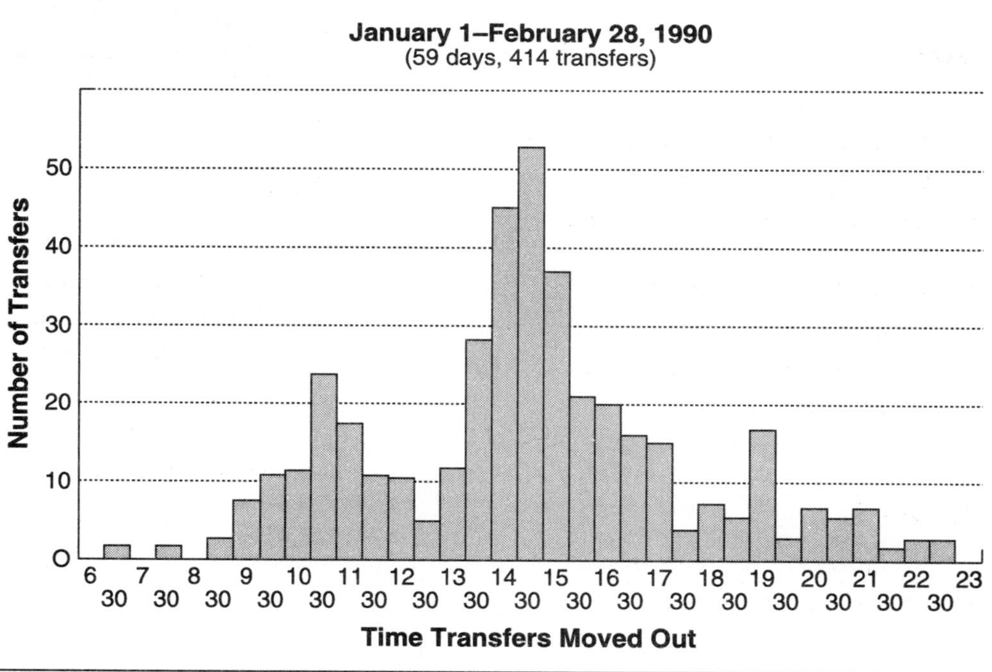

Figure 7-2 *The distribution in this histogram indicates that transfer times are unpredictable.*

Source: Bellin Health Systems, Green Bay, WI. Used with permission.

Cause-and-Effect Diagram: Patient Transfer Delays

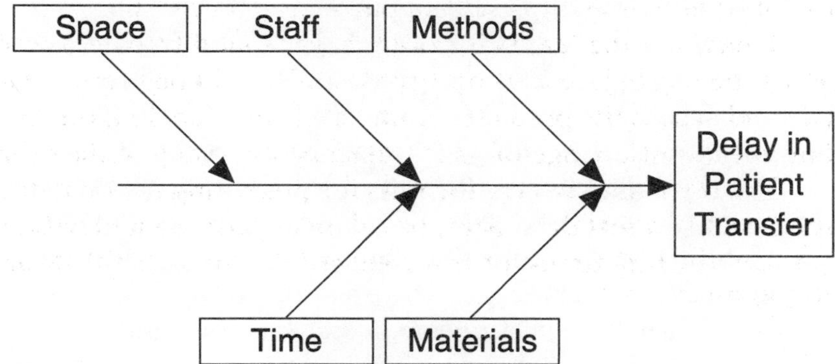

Space

- Lack of beds or private rooms
- Unexpected admissions
- Wrong sex in room
- Lack of appropriate roommate
- Patient condition
- Keeping beds for expected admission
- Waiting for discharge of another patient

Staff

- Lack of RNs
- Housekeeping staff unavailable (timely)
- Locating receiving RN
- Unexpected admission—receiving or transferring areas
- Lunch, break, supper times
- Delay in physician rounds to get orders
- Physician orders private room
- Inadequate transport staff
- Slow response from transport—lag time

Materials

- Wheelchairs/charts not available
- Obtain equipment from Central Service

Methods

- Variations in number of transfers
- Charting—excess paperwork
- RN to transport patient
- Reporting—taping
- Communication breakdown
- Unexpected admissions take priority over transfers
- Holding beds for scheduled admissions
- Delays secondary to physician orders/protocols
- Lack of policy/protocol

Time

- Time of transfer
- Time order obtained
- Time bed is available
- Time for receiving RN to get report
- Shipping time
- Shift change/personnel time
- 8- to 12-hour shift differences

Figure 7-3 *In this diagram, causes leading to transfer delays are grouped into five major categories.*

Source: Bellin Health Systems, Green Bay, WI. Used with permission.

addition, it included planning and cooperation between CCU and IMCU and 2-South. In short, it is a logical, proactive process.

The flowchart in Figure 7-4 (page 125) shows this new process.

Learn by Testing the Remedy

The team decided to pilot test the new process for 19 days. During the test, the team collected data to determine the timeliness of transfers. Figures 7-5 (page 126) and 7-6 (page 127) show the results. Figure 7-5 shows that transfer time has become much more predictable; most transfers fall within the specified time ranges. However, the graph also shows a number of transfers during the late-afternoon and early evening hours. The data also show that the formula used to predict number of transfers is accurate.

Based on these results, the team added another transfer slot—this one for after 7:00 PM. Data subsequently collected over 22 days show even more symmetry in the distribution of transfer times.

The team expected that other adjustments would be necessary based on continued monitoring.

Understand the Impact of Implementing the Remedy

The team continued to meet. Information from the team helped indicate the new process's effects and determine necessary adjustments. These effects and adjustments include the following:

- **Effect.** Valuable nursing time is wasted in packing patient belongings and transferring the patient, leading to delays in patient transfer.
- **Adjustment.** Expand the role of transport personnel to assist in gathering patient's belongings, transferring, and settling the patient.
- **Effect.** Staff are not grasping the importance of designated transfer times.
- **Adjustment.** Educate and reinforce the designated transfer times.
- **Effect.** Difficulty transferring patients by 10:30 AM.
- **Adjustment.** Extend the morning transfer time to 11 AM.

The aggregate results of the new process encouraged the team to proceed with full implementation.

Flowchart: Revised Patient Transfer Process

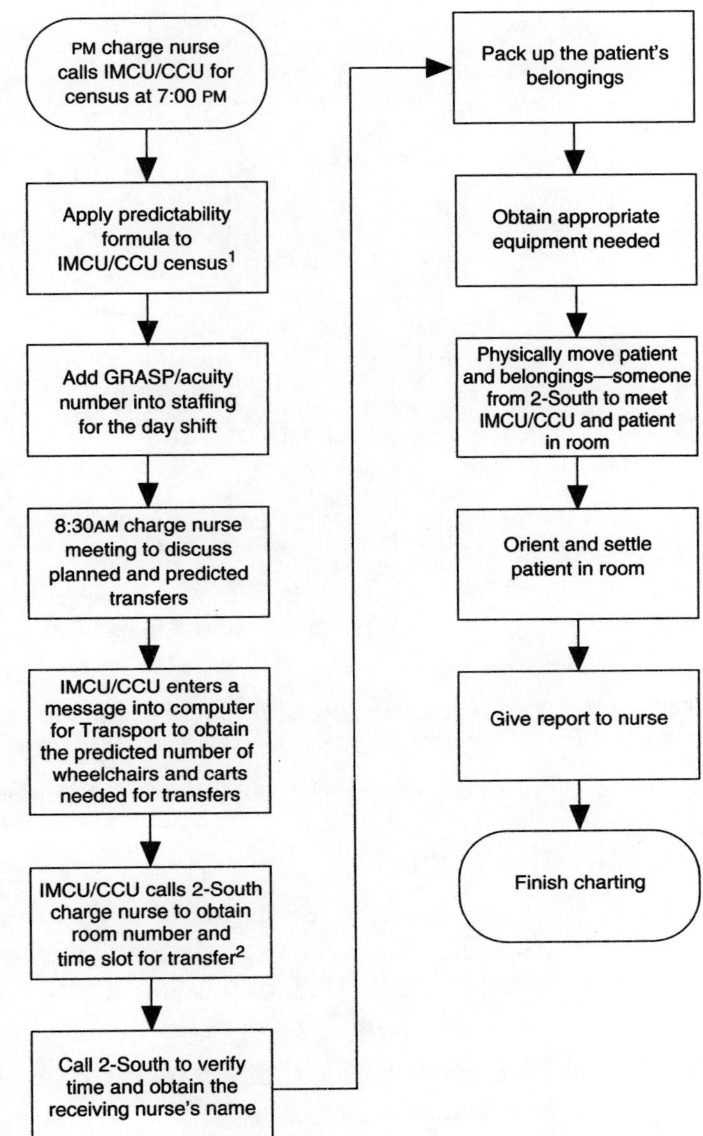

[1] The predictability formula estimates the total predicted transfers to 2-South for the next day;

- Multiply IMCU/CCU census by the respective predictability percentage to estimate the total predicted transfers;
- Take half the total predicted number of transfers;
- Round up; and
- Assign a GRASP/acuity number for each transfer to increase staffing levels.

[2] Ideally at least half the predicted transfers will occur in the morning.

Figure 7-4 *This flowchart illustrates the first revision of the patient transfer process. The graphic display shows the streamlined nature of this process in comparison with the previous process.*

Source: Bellin Health Systems, Green Bay, WI. Used with permission.

Histogram: CCU/IMCU Transfers to 2-South—Revised Process

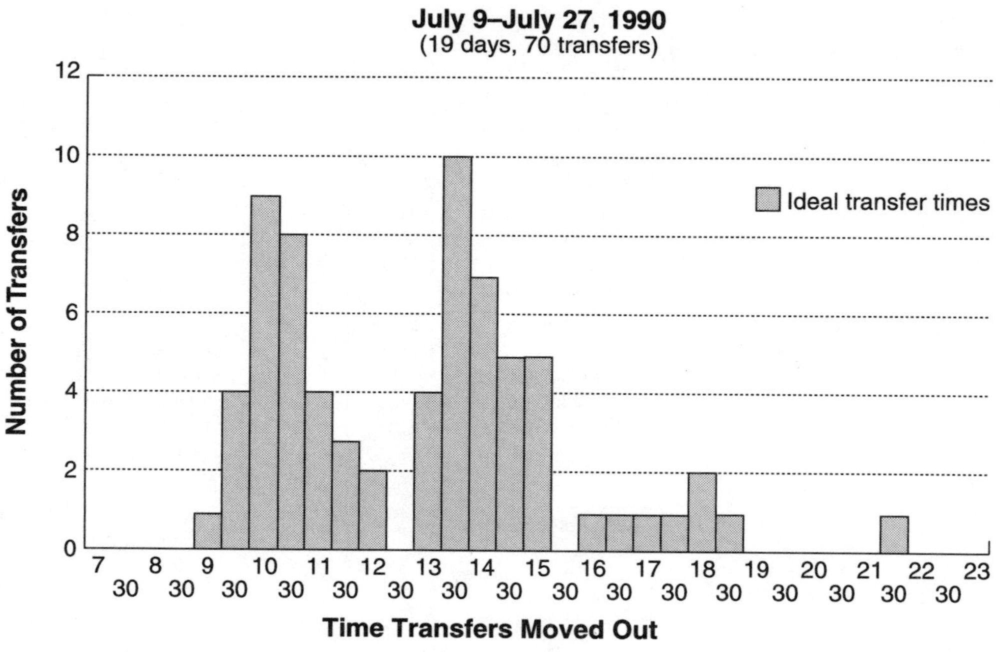

Figure 7-5 *This histogram shows the new variation distribution in transfer times resulting from the revised process. Variation is still skewed.*

Source: Bellin Health Systems, Green Bay, WI. Used with permission.

Solidify the Change

To maintain the gains achieved so far, the team worked to do the following:

- Replace the old policy and procedure for transferring a patient between CCU/IMCU and 2-South with the new transfer process. Figure 7-6 shows the final transfer process.
- Remove barriers for discussion between CCU/IMCU and 2-South staff.
- Continue to review data to determine whether the units are holding the improvement gain. This review includes developing a survey card completed for each patient transfer; the card is used to identify causes of transfer delays. The survey results are shared with staff.

The run chart in Figure 7-7 (page 128) shows the long-term performance of the patient-transfer process, starting before the team's formation and continuing well past the team's actions. This run chart shows impressive success: Originally, from 30% to less than 50% of transfers occurred in the appropriate time slots. Currently, the rate hovers near 80%.

Flowchart: Patient Transfer Process—Second Revision

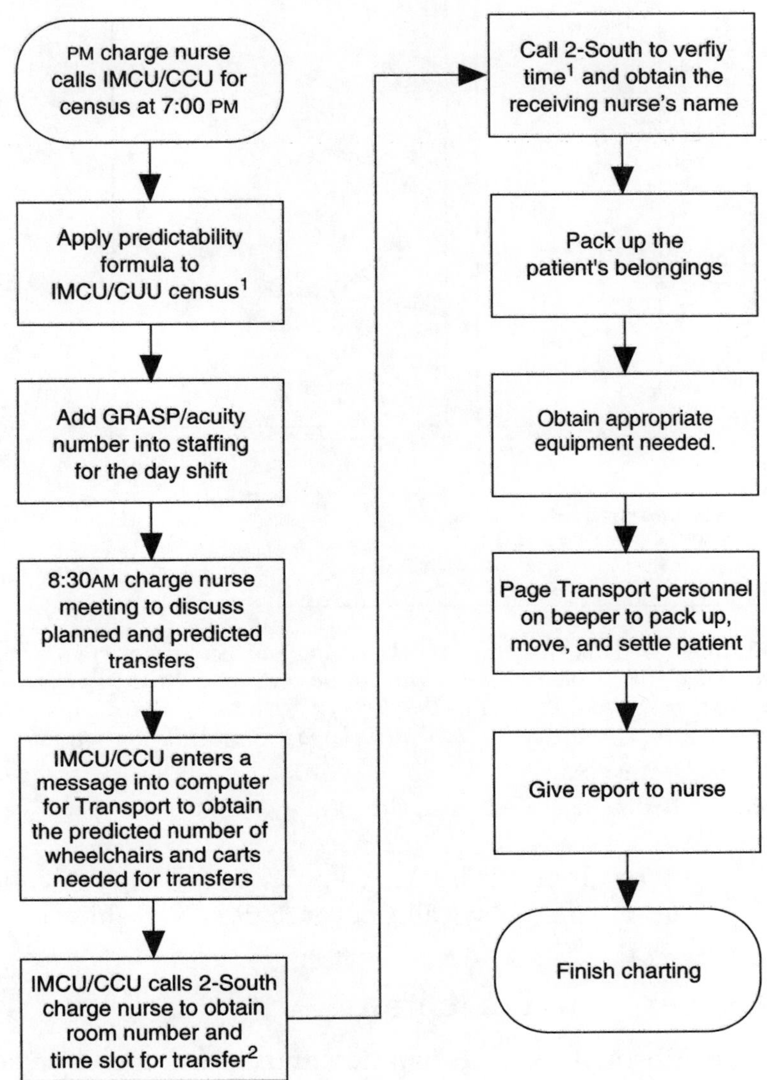

[1] The predictability formula estimates the total predicted transfers to 2-South for the next day;

- Multiply IMCU/CCU census by the respective predictability percentage to estimate the total predicted transfers;
- Take half the total predicted number of transfers;
- Round up; and
- Assign a GRASP/acuity number for each transfer to increase staffing levels.

[2] Ideally at least half the predicted transfers will occur in the morning.

Figure 7-6 *The subsequent revision of the patient transfer process is documented in this flowchart. Changes were made based on tests of the initial revision of the process.*

Source: Bellin Health Systems, Green Bay, WI. Used with permission.

Run Chart: Performance Before and After Interventions

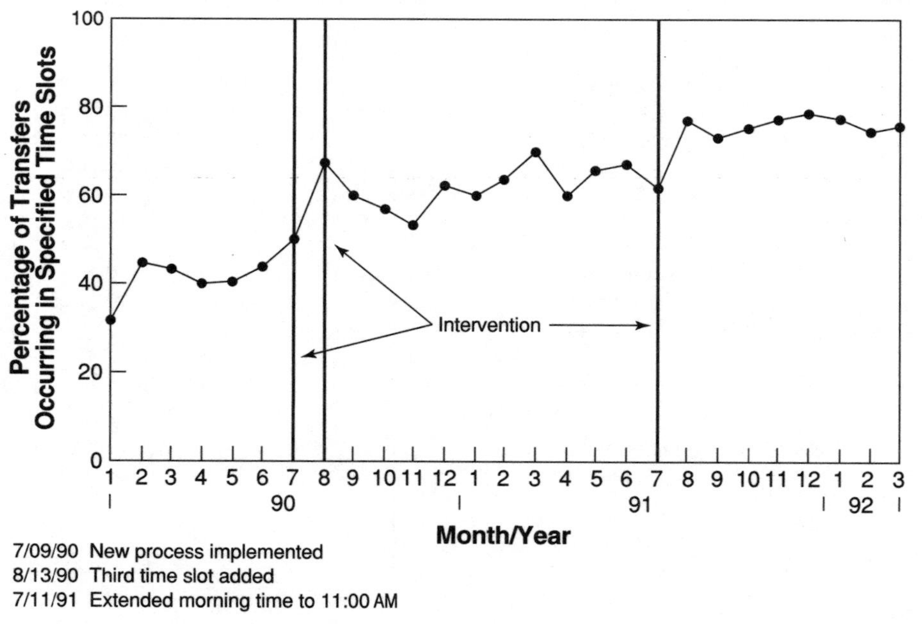

Figure 7-7 *This run chart tracks the percentage of transfers occurring within the specified time slots over a 27-month period. Before the improvement team took action, performance was in the 30% to 50% range. With each intervention, performance improved notably. In the last 8 months shown here, performance stayed near 80%.*

Source: Bellin Health Systems, Green Bay, WI. Used with permission.

As a result of this improved process, staffing difficulties, patient backlogs, and transfer delays all improved demonstrably.

Recognize and Celebrate

Bellin Hospital views recognition and celebration as critical parts of the quality improvement process. The team needed to congratulate itself on a job well done and to share the results. The celebration took the form of lunch with the team, the senior vice president, and the vice president of the nursing service; a presentation of the project at a national conference; and additional time to celebrate while at the national conference.

The team and hospital note important benefits beyond a more efficient transfer process. They discovered that the improvement process is fun for those involved, not a chore to be dreaded. They saw improved relations among departments, including departments that had previously viewed one another with suspicion. And the hospital and team were gratified to see communication barriers removed, resulting in greater cooperation and improved morale.

Conclusion

In this example, quality improvement tools were used extensively. The team used flowcharts at three different stages: first to document the original transfer procedure, then to illustrate the revised process, and finally to show the process as it was revised after tests. The team also used histograms extensively to understand the distribution of transfer times. A cause-and-effect diagram organized the many possible reasons for delays and gave the team a means to focus its improvement efforts. A run chart effectively illustrated performance over time.

The Station Call Project

CPC Valle Vista Health System is a private, 96-bed, full-service psychiatric and chemical dependency facility located in Greenwood, Indiana. The facility's leaders used W. Edwards Deming's teachings, including his famous 14 points to help shape the facility's approach to performance improvement. The facility's infrastructure for performance improvement, including its "function teams," is shown in Figure 7-8 (page 130).

The assessment function team, one of nine function teams, used performance improvement techniques and tools to help improve the process related to incoming telephone calls (called *station calls*) from people in the community who needed assistance with psychiatric and chemical dependency issues.

A station call is normally directed to the facility's access center. A call is designated a station call when an access center staff person is unavailable to take the call. The call's purpose could range from a simple question about hours of a support group meeting to a more critical "crisis" call, which requires immediate intervention. A person responding to a station call must be prepared to respond to this range of needs and to engage the services of other clinical staff, if warranted.

The Team

Forming the team to address this process and defining the team's purpose were not difficult. An existing group of professionals from various disciplines (the access center meeting members) included the necessary key players to study and improve the station call process. The team identified the following purpose: to explore the station call system to determine whether improvements could be made.

The team suspected that incoming phone calls were being missed, "lost," and not handled properly. The manager of the access center was the team leader and facilitator, with the facility's performance improvement director offering assistance with using improvement tools.

Organizational Structure for Performance Improvement

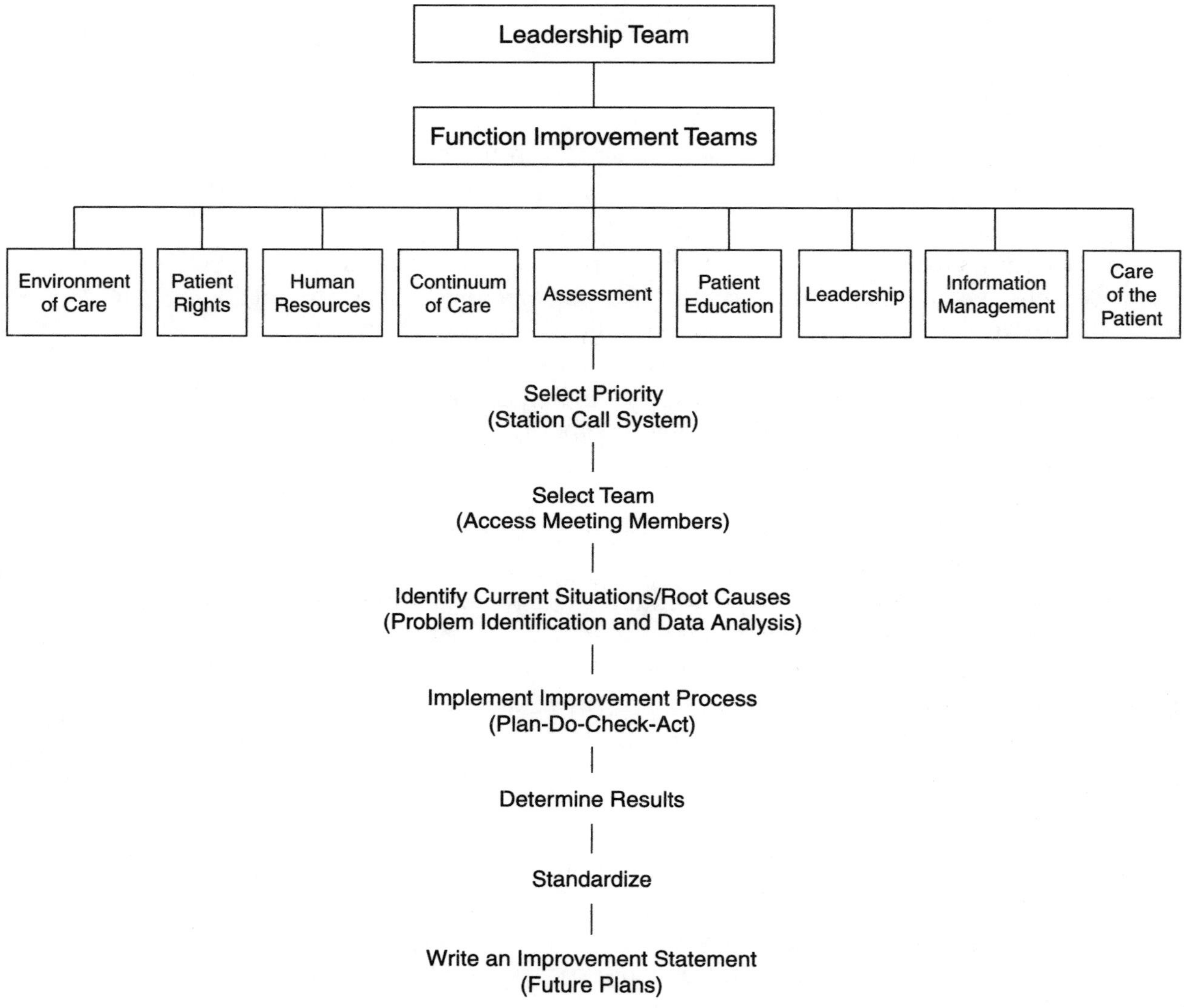

Figure 7-8 *This chart shows the improvement teams at CPC Valle Vista Health System. The teams are designated by function, and each team chooses processes within that function that are priorities for improvement. The station call project is within the assessment function.*

Source: Sheila Mishler, MSN, RNCS, and Joan Maroney, RN, CPHQ, CPC Valle Vista Health System, Greenwood, IN. Used with permission.

The team's core members included representatives from the following:

- The access center,
- Utilization management,
- Marketing,
- The admission office/reception, and
- Nursing services (supervisors and representatives of acute care units).

When necessary, the team asked others to attend meetings or provide input. These individuals are referred to as advisors. Advisors for the station call team included Valle Vista's chief executive officer and leadership team members.

Current Situation and Root Causes

To better understand the station calls issue, the team created a flowchart (see Figure 7-9, page 132). The team believed that this chart would educate them about the current process, would demonstrate possible causes of current performance, and would spur ideas for making the process more efficient and successful.

Another of the team's early steps was to create a cause-and-effect diagram (see Figure 7-10, page 133) to help clarify the possible causes of difficulties with the current process. The team chose five major categories for the causes: staff, time, callers, procedure, and materials. Key causes identified included unavailable staff, unknowledgeable staff, lack of policy, and communication breakdown.

The team also discussed how callers should be treated, whether emergency situations were handled appropriately, and whether the responses to the calls provided a positive view of Valle Vista within the community.

Based on the flowchart, cause-and-effect diagram, and other assessment, the team chose the following main categories for improving the station call process:

- Timeliness of answering calls; and
- Quality in handling the phone conversation.

Improvement

The team developed an action plan based on review of available data. The flowchart and cause-and-effect diagram had helped target potential problem areas. Actions taken can be divided into two categories: process actions and staff education. All actions were tested for limited periods of time; data were collected and assessed before more permanent implementation.

Flowchart: Station Call Process

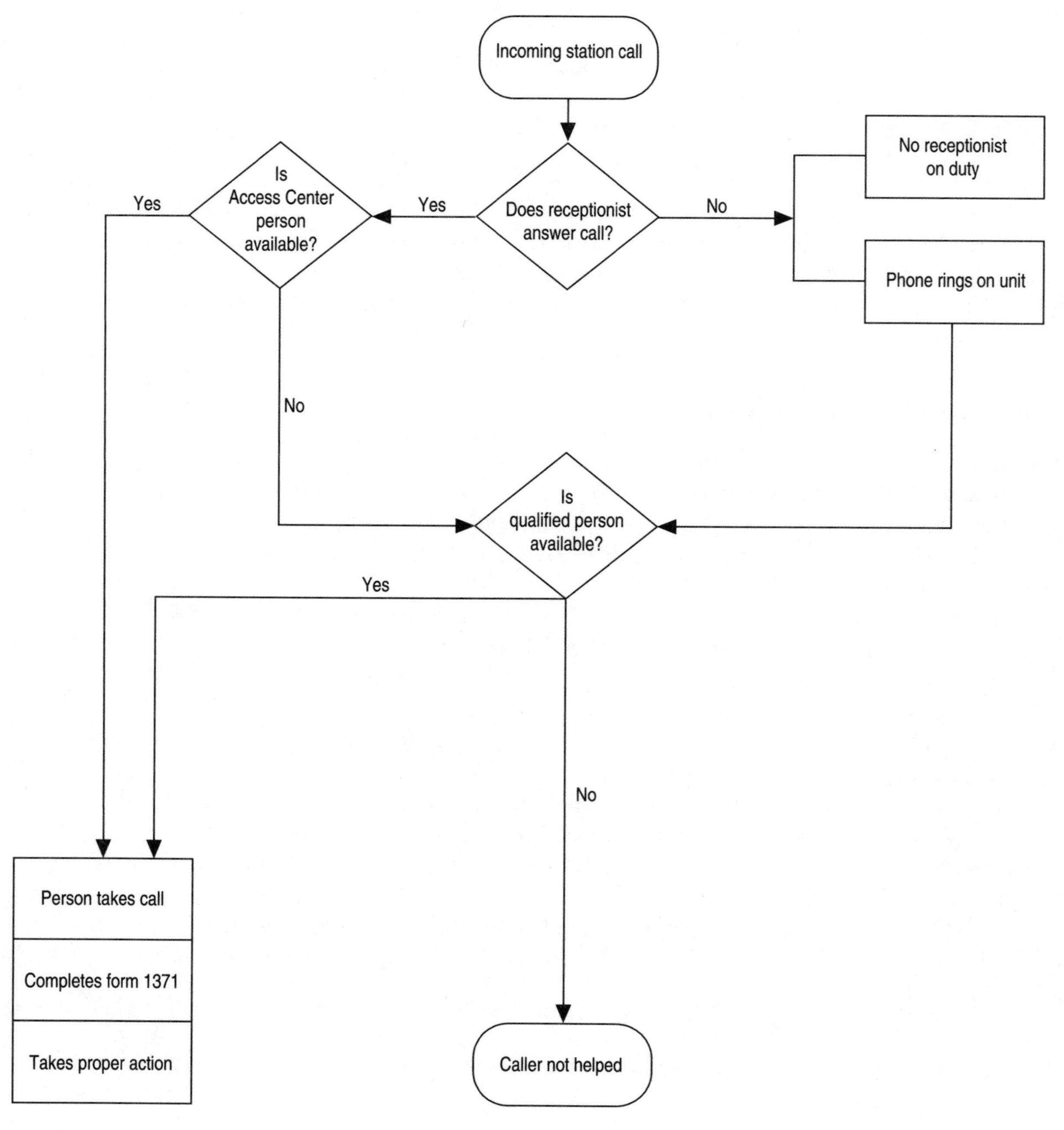

Figure 7-9 *This flowchart is a starting point for understanding the process to be improved. Problem areas are all instances in which a decision point results in a "no."*

Source: Sheila Mishler, MSN, RNCS, and Joan Maroney, RN, CPHQ, CPC Valle Vista Health System, Greenwood, IN. Used with permission.

Cause-and-Effect Diagram: Delayed or Missed Station Calls

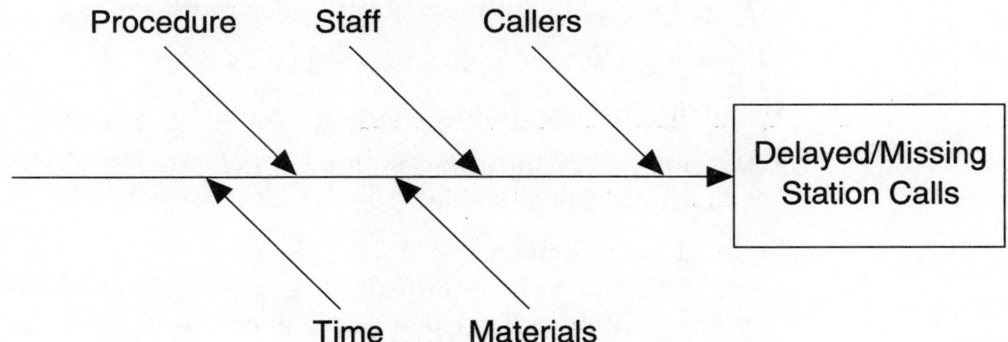

Staff

Lack of clinicians
- High turnover
- On vacation
- Outside activities
  - Marketing
  - Educational session
  - Offsite duties

Staff unavailable
- Doing paperwork
- Caring for patients
- On break
- On outing
- At lunch
- In group
- Takedown activity
- Attending meeting
- In consult/interview
  - Family/patient
  - Physician
  - Case manager

Staff not knowledgeable
- Not trained
- Unaware of importance
- No in-services

Procedure

Lack of policy
Delay secondary to protocol
No documentation guidelines
Caregivers only answer calls
Communication breakdown

Materials

Page system poor
Phone unavailable
No designated space
Reception desk delays
No resource materials
1371 forms unavailable

Time

Time of day
Staff think they're too busy
Weekend issue

Callers

Impatient: hang up phone
Change mind

Figure 7-10 *The team generated a long list of possible causes for delayed response to or missed station calls. These causes were grouped in the following categories: procedure, staff, callers, time, and materials.*

Source: Sheila Mishler, MSN, RNCS, and Joan Maroney, RN, CPHQ, CPC Valle Vista Health System, Greenwood, IN. Used with permission.

Process actions included the following:

- Generating a back-up call system;
- Making responsibility for station calls more explicit;
- Creating a written policy for the process;
- Making changes in the receptionist's role in the process; and
- Developing an "information binder" to be passed along to the assigned responsible party.

Staff education actions included the following:

- Involving nonclinical (but specifically trained) employees to answer station calls, which would allow more people to answer the calls;
- Making in-service education programs mandatory, with topics related to the station call procedure, what is expected of those handling calls, how to document calls, how to make referrals, how to handle crisis calls, and others; and
- Increasing awareness of the importance of handling station calls in a timely and proper manner.

To determine the effect of actions taken, the team chose to use two monitoring methods. The team collected data about the accountability and timeliness of station call handling for individual staff members, making ongoing reports to each individual's supervisor. In addition, the team used an outside firm to perform occasional test calls that followed established criteria. The firm provided feedback on these calls to staff, focusing on matters such as manner in which the phone was answered, triage, overall staff effectiveness, and additional comments.

Assessing Results

To display the effect of these actions on timeliness, the team used a run chart that showed not only current performance, but the previous year's performance as well (see Figure 7-11, page 135). This chart shows significant improvement in performance related to timeliness.

The bar chart in Figure 7-12 (page 135) shows the results of the efforts to improve the quality of call responses (according to the rating system developed as part of the improvement effort). This bar chart compares current performance and the past year's performance on a month-by-month basis. With the exception of one month, the current year's performance has consistently been superior to the previous year's performance.

These two display tools are clear, compelling methods for showing ongoing performance and for demonstrating improvement.

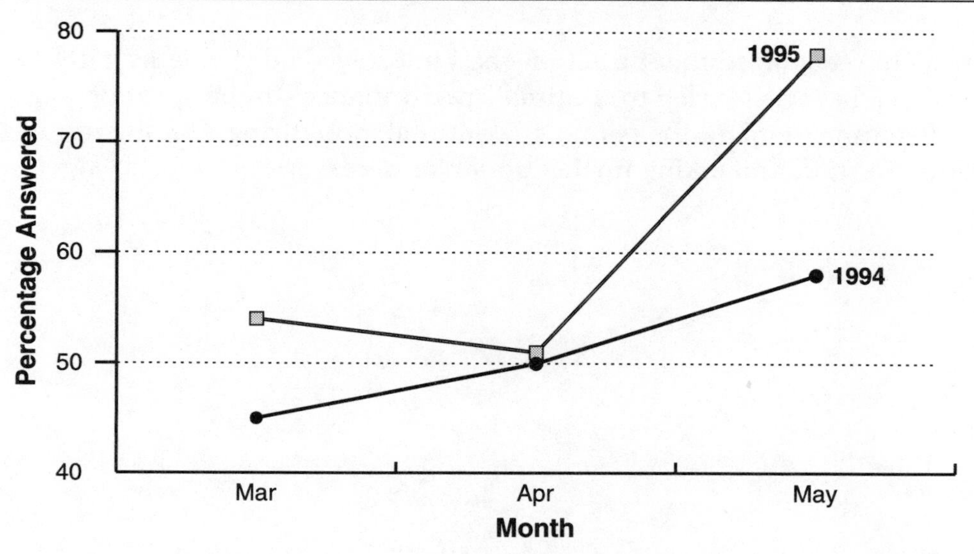

Figure 7-11 *This run chart shows the percentage of calls answered during a two-month period. The chart superimposes 1994 and 1995 performance, with significant improvement shown between April and May of 1995.*

Source: Sheila Mishler, MSN, RNCS, and Joan Maroney, RN, CPHQ, CPC Valle Vista Health System, Greenwood, IN. Used with permission.

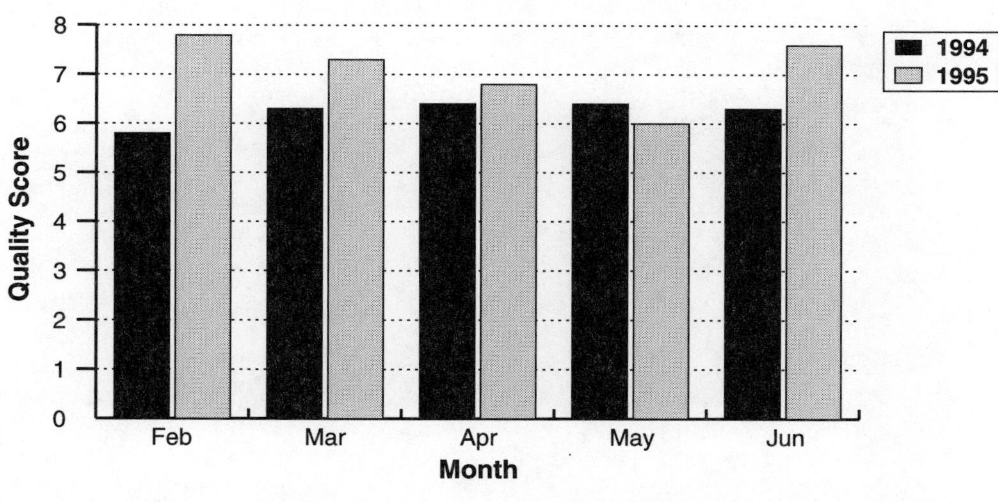

Figure 7-12 *This bar chart compares the quality of call response between February and June in 1994 and 1995. The "quality score" is assigned according to a predetermined rating system.*

Source: Sheila Mishler, MSN, RNCS, and Joan Maroney, RN, CPHQ, CPC Valle Vista Health System, Greenwood, IN. Used with permission.

Conclusion

The team recognized that its actions had not solved all problems with the station call process or led to "optimal" performance. In the spirit of continuous improvement, the team will continue monitoring, feeding information to staff, and taking further action as necessary.

Section 8 Exercise—Tracking Medical Records

In this section, readers are invited to practice the improvement tools described in this book. The section traces an improvement project at a hypothetical hospital from problem identification through analysis, action, and follow-up.

At key points in this case study, readers will find exercises they can do to improve their skills in brainstorming, multivoting, flowcharting, creating cause-and-effect diagrams, and using other tools. These exercises are best done by small groups, because most improvement initiatives are carried out by teams.

The Case

This is a fictional organization. Any resemblance to a real organization is coincidental. Ed.

University Medical Center (UMC) is a 500-bed hospital in the Midwest and has been a cornerstone of the community for many years. Margaret Smith, the CEO, is a competent and forward-thinking leader. Her institution has been using performance improvement techniques for a number of years, and continuous improvement is a key part of the institution's vision and practice.

The medical center has 300 medical staff members. The main hospital complex has three buildings: the main hospital, a professional office and classroom building, and a large ambulatory care clinic building. The medical records are kept in the basement of the main hospital. All records are hand-carried to each location in the hospital when needed.

This morning, Smith received some disturbing news. The Joint Commission had recently surveyed the hospital and had given UMC a Type I recommendation related to the medical record standards. This problem was serious, and Smith wanted to correct it immediately.

Smith decided to get to the bottom of the medical record problem personally. She had heard grumbling for years about little problems with the medical records—the physicians never signed off on them in a timely or complete manner, sometimes a chart was missing or not found where it should have been kept, there was a backlog of laboratory and x-ray reports to file on charts—but in Smith's mind, all these things were just part of running a hospital; they were never serious enough to address until now.

The Medical Records Department Perspective

Smith arrived unannounced in the office of the medical records director, James Hanson. In view of the recent survey results, Hanson was not surprised to see his CEO. In fact, he was relieved to finally have the chance to bring this problem to light.

Hanson reviewed for Smith how the Joint Commission had assessed medical records. The surveyor had reviewed selected charts against a set of criteria outlined in Joint Commission standards and the hospital's own policies. Charts that did not meet the review criteria were deemed deficient. Because 50% of the charts reviewed were deficient, a Type I recommendation had been issued.

Hanson explained to Smith that the surveyors had requested a sample of charts for the coronary bypass patients discharged over the last three months. Some of these charts were found, but not enough were found in time for the surveyor to have the sample size requested. In addition, of the charts reviewed for all the requested diagnoses and time frames, many contained deficiencies such as no history and physical, unsigned verbal orders, no operative or discharge reports, missing laboratory or x-ray reports, and so forth. Hanson apologized for the mess. He had tried his best, he said, and asked Smith if she wanted his resignation.

Smith assured Hanson that she wanted to help solve the problem and not place blame. She asked Hanson to start at the beginning and tell her why so many charts were missing. Hanson explained that controlling charts was becoming more difficult. The problem actually begins, he told her, while the chart is still on the unit. The residents are responsible for dictating a discharge summary and they need the chart for this dictation. Although the charts are supposed to be returned to the medical records department within 24 hours of discharge, the medical record technicians often need several days to find the charts. The charts are often found in the resident on-call rooms. Also, the attending physicians are likely to have the charts when they see the patients in the outpatient clinic for follow-up, and on several occasions the charts have been found there after being missing for many weeks.

Once the charts are back in the medical records department, physicians sign them out for a variety of patient-care and research reasons; however, the chart-locater system does not have enough detail in the database to record why charts are needed, exactly where they are, or who has them. Once a chart is checked out, the borrower has no incentive to return it quickly.

In addition, Hanson continued, when a patient is readmitted, the old volumes of the chart are sent up to the unit. When the Joint Commission was here, he said, some charts were on the units, some were in research or clinic offices, and some were just not where they were supposed to be.

Hanson told Smith that he did not have the staff to physically run all over the medical center looking for charts. He reminded her that his request for more staff had been denied and that he was faced with high turnover because of stress caused by the physicians not following the rules he had set to keep track of these records. Of course, he also felt that the nurses were to blame because they left medical records on the units after patients were discharged. This was true, he said, in both the inpatient units and the outpatient clinics.

Hanson went on to explain the deficiency problem. The medical records department keeps track of incomplete charts. It determines which attending physician or resident is responsible for the deficiency by reviewing the chart. Medical records staff send letters to the responsible parties, reminding them to dictate or sign orders or reports; the charts are then placed in the physician's file in the physicians' dictation room, a small room next to the medical records department and the physicians' lounge. The medical records department has attempted to put sanctions on the physicians, but the sanctions just don't work.

Smith thanked Hanson for his candor and decided to gather more information on the problem from the medical director.

The Medical Staff Perspective

Smith left the medical records department and walked directly to the office of the vice president of the medical staff, Helen Riley. Riley shook her head when she heard about the Type I recommendation from the Joint Commission. The deficiency and availability problems are the same issue, she told Smith. The physicians try to sign reports or dictate, but the charts can't be found, or the physicians' dictation room has no space or phones. "How can they do the charts in this room?" she asked. "It's impossible. Also, the medical records department is wrong all the time about who is deficient. Often the deficiency letter is for a case the physician has already cleared up or for a case the physician receiving the letter is not responsible for. These mistakes get the physicians angry and they occur so often that the physicians don't pay attention to the notices anymore. Also, the physicians have no one from medical records they can talk to about the problem."

While on the subject of medical records, Riley had a few other issues that needed to be addressed. She told Smith that the nursing and clerical staff on the units handle records very poorly, and, frankly, she had concerns about patient confidentiality. The records are not kept in a consistent place on each unit. Old charts from previous stays are usually thrown in a drawer, if they can be found at all. And the clerks don't file laboratory reports in a timely manner on the current patient chart.

Finally, far too many records were in the performance-improvement office for its use. Riley was adamant that these functions caused more problems with the medical records and created more work than the functions were worth.

The Finance Department Perspective

Smith walked back to her office and found the director of finance, Bob Brown, waiting for her. The peer review organization had just informed him that it would not reimburse the medical center for cases in which no medical record could be found and even wanted repayment for cases that had already been reimbursed. In addition, if charts that had been reviewed or the required document signed by the physician attesting to the correct diagnosis were missing, no reimbursements would be issued.

Brown admitted that the missing documents might be partly his fault. Finance cannot cut a Medicare invoice until billing information is released by medical records staff after the document is signed. He had been leaning on the director of medical records to release billing information faster, but it seems that pressure made the medical records department omit some steps in its process.

An Improvement Initiative

Smith sat back in her chair. How had things gotten so out of control? None of these problems was new. They had been addressed in the past, but the issues always seemed to creep back. The medical center had successfully used improvement teams to address such difficulties in the past. The problems with medical records and the Type I recommendation made the issue a high priority.

Exercise One: Choosing Team Members

Smith formed a task force of key people to work on the medical records problem. Who do you think should be included in this task force? Write your answer here. The task force can have any number of members you deem appropriate:

- ______________________________
- ______________________________
- ______________________________
- ______________________________

- ____________________________________
- ____________________________________
- ____________________________________
- ____________________________________

Exercise Two: Brainstorming and Multivoting

At the task force's first meeting, it held brainstorming and multivoting sessions to determine the issues about medical records that needed attention. Review the method for brainstorming in Section 3 (pages 37–39). Then, in a small group, take 10 minutes to brainstorm the issue. First, list the responses from each person on a large sheet of paper or a flip chart; then multivote to decide the most important medical records issue at this hospital. Take 20 minutes to do this exercise.

List your top five issues here:

1. ____________________________________
2. ____________________________________
3. ____________________________________
4. ____________________________________
5. ____________________________________

Exercise Three: Creating a Flowchart

The medical center's task force identified these issues in its brainstorming and multivoting exercise:

1. Missing records and records not easily found;
2. Records not accessible to staff for completing deficiencies;
3. Security/confidentiality of record not protected;
4. Competing need for the record between medical records, billing, clinical staff; and
5. Noncompliance with medical records department rules.

The task force chose to look at the first problem and to focus on the tracking issue because the members believed that (1) the missing record issue was the most critical problem to resolve and (2) many of the other problems may have resulted from this one issue.

In your group, create a flowchart illustrating the medical record flow process from discharge of an inpatient to the record being filed as complete in the medical records department. Work from a high-level flowchart to a more detailed chart. Include a call for the medical record to an outpatient or emergency department area for a patient visit post-discharge, and include the flow process for a record review for performance-improvement activities.

If your group members have significantly different ideas about the way the process works, it means the process is not clear or consistently performed in the organization. Use the majority-rules method to decide the most frequently used approach to the process.

Stop after the flowchart is complete.

Exercise Four: Creating a Cause-and-Effect Diagram

After reviewing your flowchart, build a cause-and-effect diagram to identify the possible causes of missing charts. Look for

- points in the process that may cause trouble,
- parts of the process you don't understand,
- steps that seem irritating or that don't make sense, and
- gaps in the process.

Try to take the diagram to as many levels of *why* as you can for each possible cause. Ask *why* at least five times to get to the possible root cause.

The task force had defined *missing record* as follows: An inpatient record not found where the medical record tracking log said it would be (for instance, the medical records department, the physicians' deficient chart area, or the inpatient unit where the patient last stayed).

The Case, Continued

Finding Root Causes

After the task force reviewed the cause-and-effect diagram, it noted several possible causes of the missing patient charts. These causes follow, along with reasons leading to the root cause:

1. Physicians take records to complete from the dictating lounge where deficient records are filed. The task force suspects that records are taken to physicians' offices or homes. Reasons include the following:

- Physicians are too busy to wait for a dictation phone. It's easier to call in on an outside line to get into dictation.
- The lounge area is too crowded.
- Physicians can't hear paging in this area.
- There are not enough phones, chairs, or desk space.
- Only three physicians can use the area at one time; physicians don't have time to wait.

2. A nursing supervisor, clinic nurse, or emergency department nurse takes the chart from the medical records area without signing it out properly because it is needed for a patient visit in outpatient services or the emergency department. Reasons include the following:
   - Staff can't wait for medical records staff to send the chart. The chart takes too long to get, and the patient visit is over before the chart arrives.
   - Nurses don't know how to sign out the record properly.
   - Only one person in the medical records department is authorized to sign out records, and the nurses either can't find or can't wait for this person.
   - The proper sign-out cards are never where they can be found, so when nursing staff take out a chart, they leave either a handwritten note that doesn't have adequate information on it or they leave no sign-out record.
   - The nurses are in too big a hurry to wait for all the paperwork to be done because the clinic needs the chart immediately.

3. Staff doesn't return the chart after signing it out, and it gets left in a clinic or the emergency department for long periods. Reasons include the following:
   - Staff (nurses, physicians, and so on) are too busy to return the records.
   - The medical records department is out of the way when the staff leave the units, and nobody wants to go to the basement to return the charts.
   - Some staff hate going to the basement. It is remote, and they don't feel safe going there, especially after hours when most clinic or emergency department shifts are over.

- There are often too many charts to carry.
- Staff tries to return the charts, but they are scattered all over and many get missed, left in rooms, or left in remote areas of the clinics or the emergency department.
- Some staff are confused about who is responsible for getting the charts back to the medical records department.

4. Chart is delayed in getting to the medical records department after discharge and gets lost prior to being sent there from the unit. Reasons include the following:
   - Medical students and residents take the charts from the units to complete assignments and case studies for class.
   - Unit clerks keep charts on the units to file the backlog of laboratory, EKG, consult, and other reports.
   - Utilization review staff take the chart to a back room or lounge area to work on it and leave it there.
   - Staff trying to tidy up the nurses' station shove charts into a drawer to get them out of the way, and the charts are forgotten.
   - The unit clerk forgets to pull a chart apart after discharge, and it stays in the rack until a new patient arrives or the night staff takes it out; the night staff doesn't always put the chart in the correct spot.
5. Too many people need the chart, and it goes to too many places. It never seems to be in the medical records department. Reasons include the following:
   - The chart is frequently at the quality improvement office.
   - The chart is often with utilization review or risk management.
   - The business office takes the chart for billing.
   - Head nurses are requested to do billing audits and often need charts.
   - Physicians need access to charts to finish deficiencies.

Collecting Data About Causes

The task force decided that it was time to use data to make decisions about the actual causes among these perceived possible causes.

A three-month study was undertaken to collect data on the causes of misplaced medical records. Operational definitions were agreed on for each cause, and a check sheet was developed to record how a chart left the medical record tracking system.

The following paragraphs offer an overview of the study.

Data were recorded and a cause was attributed to a lost record in one of three scenarios:

1. A record was requested (or located) that was not found where the medical record tracking system said it would be. In such a case, the check sheet recorded the last known official location of the record, because the record was assumed to have been taken or lost at this point.

2. The record was not listed as entering the medical record tracking system as of the second day after patient discharge. Medical records staff compared the charts returned to the discharge list daily to collect these data.

3. A record was returned to the department when that record was not documented as being anywhere other than in the medical record's permanent file. Under these circumstances, it was assumed that the record had been taken and not signed out.

The assistant director of the department was assigned to help organize this study for the three-month period. Although he did not work full time on this project, he did spend time coordinating the data for the period. The staff used check sheets for the data collection.

Figures 8-1 through 8-3 (pages 146–148) show the resulting check sheets.

Analyzing the Results of Data Collection

The numerical data from the check sheets were put into a Pareto chart for the task force to analyze. This chart ranked the number of lost charts for the various points of loss (see Figure 8-4, page 149). This diagram showed that the most common point of loss was the physicians' deficient filing area; the second most common was outpatient services; and the emergency department and the medical records department were tied for the third most common point of loss.

The task force suspected that three of these areas—the emergency department, outpatient services, and the medical records department—were related. Therefore, the task force created another Pareto chart combining these three into one. This chart also showed that the physicians' deficient filing area was the most common point of loss. The task force decided to work on this aspect of the problem first.

Check Sheet 1

Month June 1996

		Totals
Signed out charts missing from		
Physician deficiency chart area	IIIIIIIIIIIIIIII	16
Head nurse's office	II	2
Pediatrics unit	I	1
5-West		
Outpatient	IIIII	5
Emergency department	IIII	4
Utilization review		
Quality improvement office		
Medical records department (not signed out)	III	3
Not returned following discharge Pediatrics	II	2
3-West	II	2
3-East	I	1

Figure 8-1 *The medical records task force used this check sheet to collect data about missing records during June. The location refers to the last recorded location of the missing or misplaced record.*

Further Evaluation

Physical description. The physicians' deficient chart filing and dictating area is located in a small room next to the main medical records department. It is separated by a small doorway that does not allow staff from the medical records department to see into the room. The filing area is a large set of shelves on which the charts are filed by physician name and a work area comprising a long table with three dictation phones and six chairs, where the physicians can complete the charts. Another doorway on the opposite side of the room leads into the main hall of the basement area.

The physicians' lounge is next to the deficient chart room, but can only be accessed by going into the main hall from the chart room. The

Check Sheet 2

Month July 1996

		Totals
Signed out charts missing from		
Physician deficiency chart area	IIIIIIIIIIIIIIII	16
Head nurse's office		
Pediatrics unit		
5-West		
Outpatient	III	3
Emergency department	III	3
Utilization review		
Quality improvement office		
Medical records department (not signed out)	III	3
Not returned following discharge Pediatrics	III	3
3-West	II	2
3-East	I	1

Figure 8-2 *The medical records task force used this check sheet to collect data about missing records during July, the second month of the three-month study.*

physicians' chart filing area and the physicians' lounge are never locked, and there are no staff in either area. Staff are in the medical records department; after 5 PM, only transcription staff are there, and they sit at the far side of the department and cannot see the physicians' filing area.

Survey and time-and-use study. The task force decided to use two methods to find out what was really happening in the deficient chart area. First it sent a survey to all the medical staff physicians asking them to explain why they thought charts were taken from this area and how this problem could be rectified.

Then a time-and-use study was done by the medical records staff over a three-day period. Staff were assigned to the filing area and collected data every hour on how many physicians were using the desk area and how many tried to use it but could not find space or telephones for dictation. It was also noted when nonphysician staff came into the room

Check Sheet 3

Month August 1996		Totals
Signed out charts missing from		
Physician deficiency chart area	IIIIIIIIIIIIIIIII	17
Head nurse's office	I	1
Pediatrics unit		
5-West		
Outpatient	II	2
Emergency department	III	3
Utilization review		
Quality improvement office		
Medical records department (not signed out)	IIII	4
Not returned following discharge Pediatrics	III	3
3-West	III	3
3-East	II	2

Figure 8-3 *The medical records task force used this check sheet to collect data about missing records during August, the third month of the three-month study.*

to access a chart. The times of occurrence as well as the number of incidents were noted.

The physician survey showed that most could not find seating or a dictation phone to use when they had time at the hospital to do their charts. They expressed anger at being expected to come in on their days off to work on these charts. They wanted time with their families, too. Many responded that they did in fact take charts home or to their office to get them done. It was easier to call in from the outside to get a dictation line than to wait in the chart room for a phone to be free, and there was never enough space to take out all the charts and work on them because the room was so crowded.

The time-and-use study done by medical records staff was graphed on a histogram, such as the one shown in Figure 8-5 (page 150). The results showed that most physicians used the room during the prime work hours and fewer used the room after work hours. Many of the physician complaints about lack of availability were proven true.

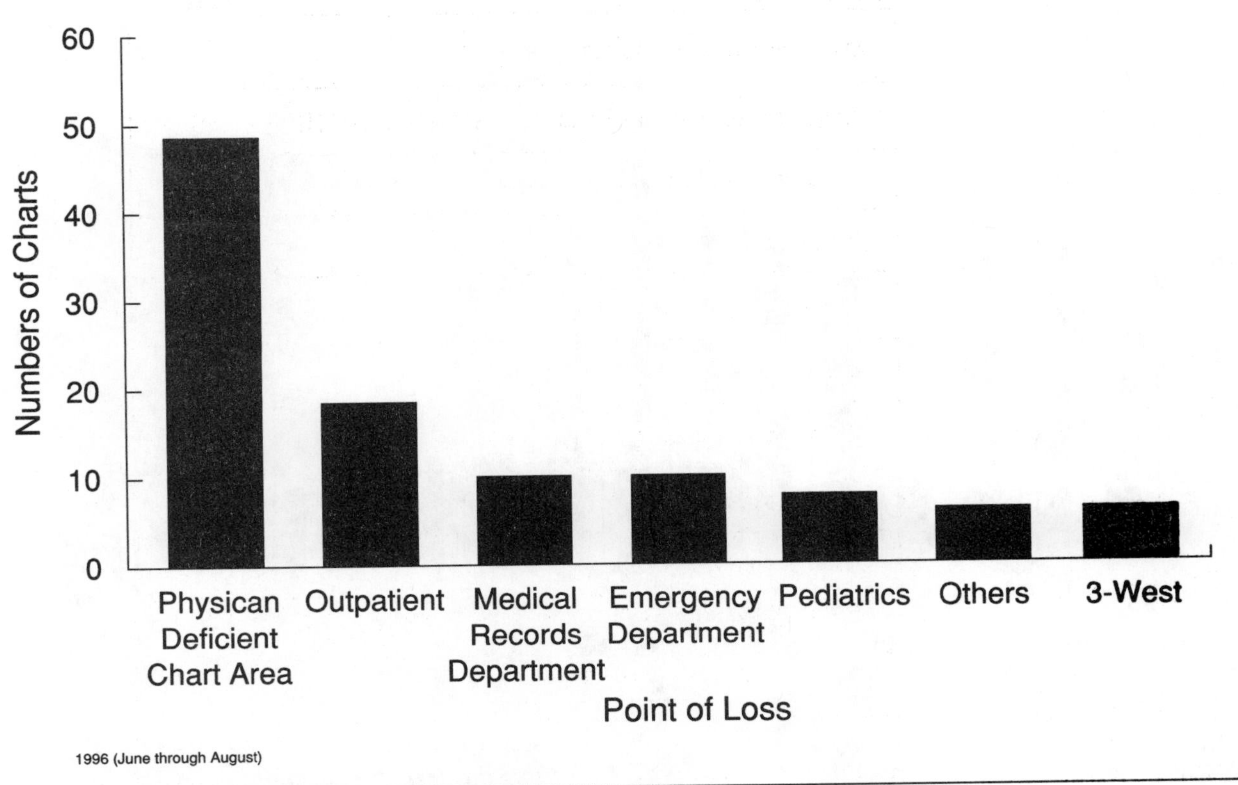

Figure 8-4 *This Pareto chart ranks the locations according to the number of missing charts lost in each.*

Taking Action

The task force proposed the following possible solutions and then developed a decision grid to choose the solution with the best chance for success:

- Gut the current room used for the physicians' filing area and replace it with a large room filled with individual dictation cubicles. Take the space from the medical records department and the physicians' lounge.
- Modify the current room by adding more tables and installing more phones. Even if it is still too crowded, at least the doctors will have the equipment to use.
- Computerize the medical record, with doctors having access codes from any hospital terminal, office, or home computer.
- Place a guard at the physicians' deficient chart room to keep charts there.

Histogram: Physician Use of Deficiency Chart Area

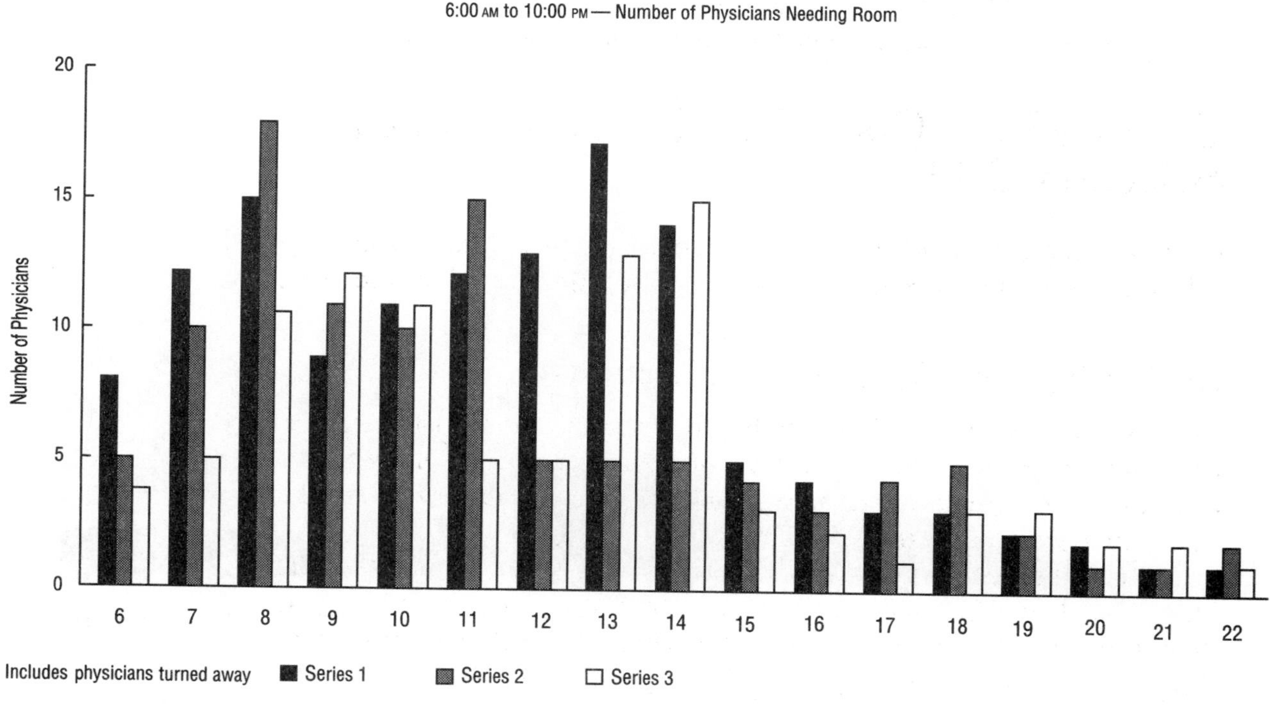

Figure 8-5 *This histogram shows the frequency with which physicians use the deficient chart area at various times between 6 AM and 10 PM. The study covers three days; each bar represents a different day.*

- Knock out the wall between the medical records department and the physicians' dictation room; put in 12 cubicles with phones, and staff the area with a medical record aide from 6 AM to 11 PM.
- Schedule times for the physicians to use the room.
- Put six additional cubicles in the physicians' lounge until a permanent solution can be found.
- [Propose your own solutions with your group.]

The task force determined these criteria for the selection grid:

- The solution must solve the usage problem by providing space for at least 12 physicians at one time;
- The solution must be of reasonable cost;
- The solution must provide help and support to physicians;
- The solution must be acceptable to physicians;
- The solution must protect the medical record;
- Short-term action must take place within 1 month;

- Long-term action must take place over the next 12 to 24 months; and
- [Propose your own criteria with your group.]

Exercise Five: Choosing a Decision Using a Selection Grid

Fill in the selection grid shown in Figure 8-6 (page 152) with the proposed solutions and criteria. Rate each proposed solution based on the criteria.

Evaluating the Effectiveness of Actions

The task force knew that it would be important to monitor the issue after the solution was in place. The following indicator was developed and monitored: "Charts listed as being in physician's file but not found there by medical records staff or physician."

The indicator's rationale was that charts assigned to the physician's file in the physicians' deficient chart and dictation room should remain there until the chart was finished, after which it should be returned to the medical records department for permanent filing.

A mechanism for collecting data was established. Data were collected and totaled monthly. Over time, the upper and lower control limits would be established. Figures 8-7 and 8-8 (page 153) show run charts displaying performance for this indicator over time. The run charts will become a control chart once the upper and lower control limits can be set.

Conclusion

This case study shows a logical, judicious approach to improving medical record tracking, using tools for creating ideas (brainstorming), for reaching consensus (multivoting and selection grid), for understanding a process (flowchart), for finding causes (cause-and-effect diagram), for collecting data (check sheet), for displaying and analyzing data (Pareto chart and histogram), and for monitoring performance (run chart and control chart).

Note that the task force identified many possible causes for lost and misplaced medical records. It did not, however, attempt to address all or even most of these causes. Instead, the task force chose the most pervasive cause—a choice based on data, not anecdotal information or impressions—and focused its efforts there. In the future, other aspects of medical record tracking could certainly be earmarked for improvement.

Selection Grid: Choosing an Improvement Action

Solution	Provide needed space	Reasonable cost	Support physicians	Acceptable to physicians	Protect medical records	Short-term action	Long-term action	Other criterion (specify)	Totals
1. Gut current room and expand.									
2. Modify current room by adding tables and phones.									
3. Computerize medical records.									
4. Place guard in room.									
5. Knock out wall between current room and medical records room.									
6. Schedule times for physicians to use the room.									
7. Add six cubicles in lounge.									
8. Propose own solution.									

(Criteria)

Figure 8-6 *As part of Exercise 5, use this selection grid to choose among the proposed actions to reduce the number of missing medical records from the physicians' deficient chart area. Use the task force's criteria to judge the effectiveness of each solution. The solution with the largest total should be considered as the first problem-solving action.*

Run Chart: Missing Charts After Corrective Action

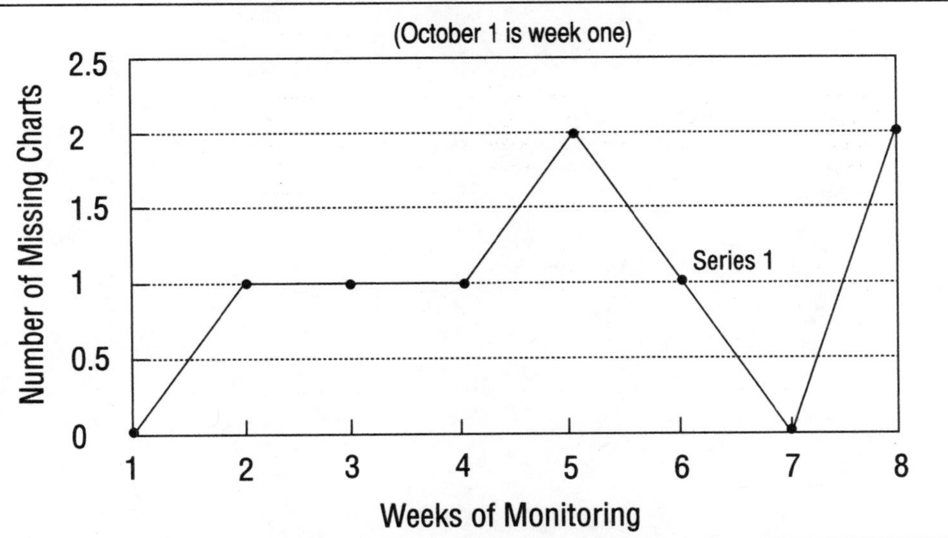

Figure 8-7 *This run chart depicts the number of missing charts after the corrective actions were implemented. Once upper and lower control limits can be set, this run chart will become a control chart that staff can use to determine whether the medical record tracking process is statistically in control or whether further action is necessary to improve the process.*

Run Chart: Before and After Corrective Action

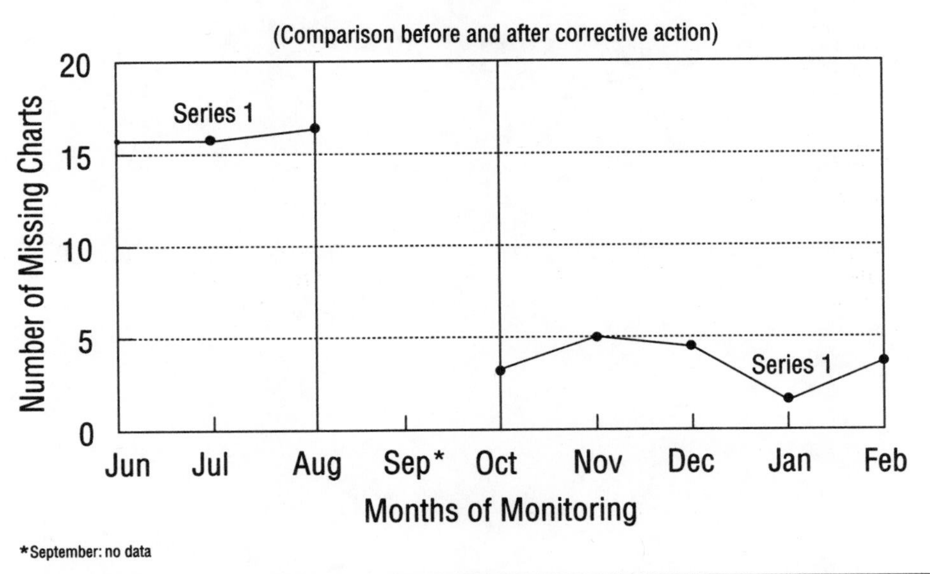

Figure 8-8 *This run chart illustrates the dramatic decrease in missing charts after the corrective actions were implemented in October.*

Appendix

Constructing Statistical Control Charts*

The following is an excerpt from Chapter 9: "Statistical Quality Control" in Quantitative Analysis for Health Services Administration *by Charles J. Austin and Stuart B. Boxerman. This appendix is offered to give readers expert advice on use of statistical control charts. Other explanations of how to construct a control chart are available from other sources.*

Statistical control charts are graphic tools for plotting performance data about established quality standards or past performance history with outliers falling outside an acceptable range of variation. Most control charts assume that the parent population of the variable being measured follows a normal probability distribution. Computer programs for producing quality control charts that make this assumption should include a statistical test of the data for normality.

Figure A-1 (page 156) depicts a normal distribution of a set of values being monitored in a quality control process. The expected value is the mean of the distribution ($\bar{x}$). Variation is measured by the standard deviation from the mean (s). For a perfect normal distribution, 68% of the variation will occur within one standard deviation from the mean, 95% will occur within two standard deviations from the mean, and 99.8% will occur within three standard deviations from the mean.

Statistical control charts are developed by taking repeated samples of a variable to be monitored over time and plotting the distribution of the sample means in reference to the average of all observations. Data values are plotted in reference to a *center* and two limits, the *upper control limit* (UCL) and the *lower*

*Used with permission from Quantitative Analysis for Health Services Administration by Charles J. Austin and Stuart B. Boxerman (Chicago: Health Administration Press, 1995), pp 200–204.

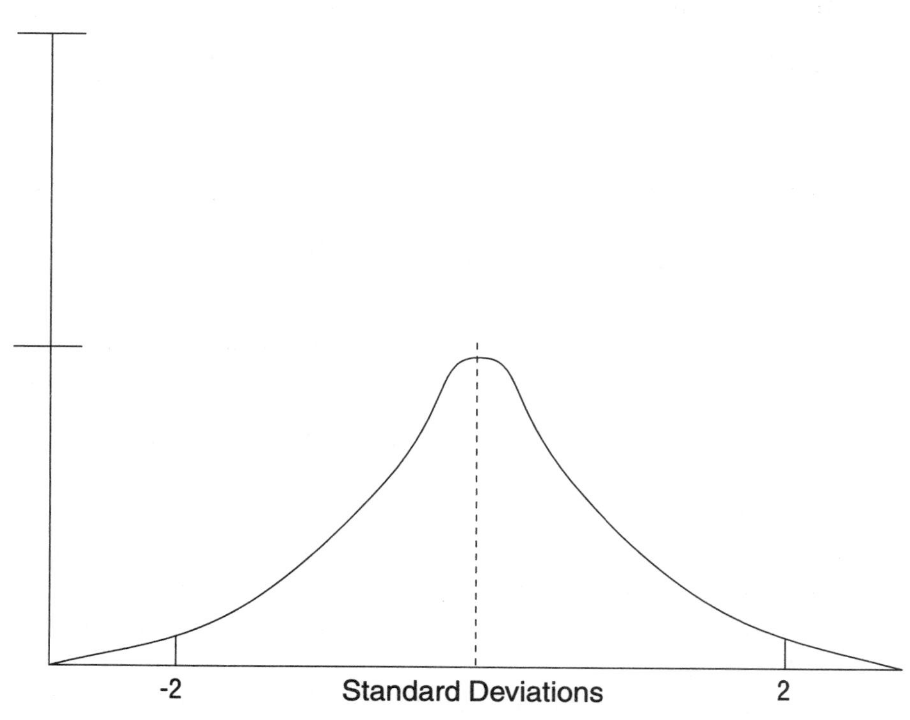

Figure A-1 *This control chart shows standard normal distribution. Used with permission from* Quantitative Analysis for Health Services Administration *by Charles J. Austin and Stuart B. Boxerman (Chicago: Health Administration Press, 1995), pp 200–204.*

control limit (LCL). The center is the grand sample mean, which is the average of the individual sample means. It is common to set control limits that are two or three standard deviations from the grand sample mean. That is, the probability of a sample mean having a value more than two (or three) standard deviations higher or lower than the mean by random chance is less than 5% (or 1%) and there is likely to be an assignable cause for the deviation.

To illustrate the construction of a control chart, consider the following simple example. The city health department operates a drop-in primary care clinic. The clinic manager has collected the following data on average waiting times for patients seeking service at the clinic. Waiting times for a sample of four patients per day have been collected for a five-day period:

Waiting Times (minutes)

Day	Patient A	Patient B	Patient C	Patient D	Mean	Range
1	25	18	23	24	22.50	7
2	32	30	26	22	27.50	10
3	14	21	20	25	20.00	11
4	20	26	16	19	20.25	10
5	18	23	25	20	21.50	7
				Total	111.75	45

A statistical control chart is constructed that plots the values of the daily means for each day in the sample (see Figure A-2, page 158). This is referred to as a *mean* or an *x-bar* chart. The center line for the chart is computed as follows:

$$\bar{\bar{X}} = \Sigma \text{ of daily means/number of days}$$

$$\bar{\bar{X}} = 111.75/5 = 22.35$$

Upper and lower control limits are established at either two or three standard deviations from the center line to provide easy visual monitoring of points on the graph that are outside these limits, or "out of control." That is, the probability of this occurring by random events is very low. The following formulas are used in constructing these control limits:

For three standard deviations:

$$UCL = \bar{\bar{X}} + 3\bar{R}/d2\sqrt{n}$$
$$LCL = \bar{\bar{X}} - 3\bar{R}/d2\sqrt{n}$$

For two standard deviations:

$$UCL = \bar{\bar{X}} + 2\bar{R}/d2\sqrt{n}$$
$$LCL = \bar{\bar{X}} - 2\bar{R}/d2\sqrt{n}$$

where

$$\bar{R} = \Sigma \text{ of daily range value/number of days}$$
$$\bar{R} = 45/5 = 9$$

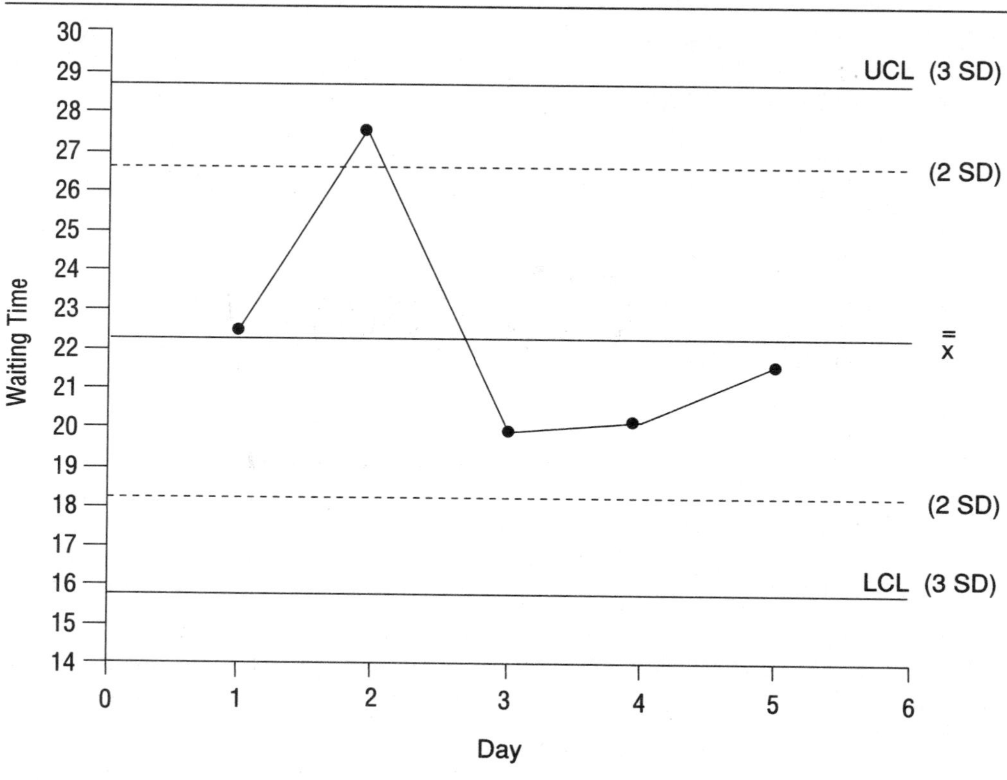

Figure A-2 *This control chart shows a mean. Used with permission from* Quantitative Analysis for Health Services Administration *by Charles J. Austin and Stuart B. Boxerman (Chicago: Health Administration Press, 1995), pp 200–204.*

n = number of patients in daily sample = 4

$d2$ = a constant value used in estimating the standard deviation = 2.1

Thus, at the three standard deviation level, the control limits are

$$UCL = 22.35 + 3(9)/2.1\sqrt{4} = 28.78$$
$$LCL = 22.35 - 3(9)/2.1\sqrt{4} = 15.92$$

And at the two standard deviation level, the control limits are

$$UCL = 22.35 + 2(9)/2.1\sqrt{4} = 26.64$$
$$LCL = 22.35 - 2(9)/2.1\sqrt{4} = 18.06$$

Note that in Figure A-2, all five daily mean waiting times fall within the upper and lower control limits at the three standard deviation level. However, the mean waiting time for Day 2 is above the two standard deviation control line, with a probability of this occurring by chance of less than 5%.

Glossary

activity network diagram (AND)*

A graphic display showing total completion time, the necessary sequence of tasks, the tasks that can be done simultaneously, and the critical tasks to monitor. Allows a team to find both the most efficient path and a realistic schedule for the completion of any project.

affinity diagram

An approach to organizing facts, opinions, and issues into natural groups by listing on cards inputs from knowledgeable people and then rearranging the cards until useful groups are identified. A display of the groups of cards that express related ideas is the affinity diagram.

appropriateness

In health care, a performance dimension addressing the degree to which the care/intervention provided is relevant to a patient's clinical needs, given the current state of knowledge.

benchmark

(1) A point of reference or standard by which something can be measured, compared, or judged, as in benchmarks of performance. (2) A standard unit for the basis of comparison, that is, a universal unit that is identified with sufficient detail so that other similar classifications can be compared as being above, below, or comparable to the benchmark.

brainstorming

A process used to elicit a large number of ideas from a group of people who are encouraged to use their collective thinking power to generate ideas and unrestrained thoughts in a relatively short period of time.

cause-and-effect diagram

A pictorial display drawn to represent the relationship between some effect and all the possible causes influencing it. Also called a fishbone diagram or an Ishikawa diagram.

check sheet

A data-collection form that helps to summarize data based on sample observations and begin to identify patterns. A check sheet is used to answer the question, How often are certain events happening? It starts the process of translating "opinions" into "facts." The completed form displays the data in a simple graphic summary.

common-cause variation

Variation in a process that is due to the process itself and is produced by interactions of variables of that process. Common-cause variation is inherent in all processes.

* Source: Brassard M, Ritter D: *The Memory Jogger* TM II: *A Pocket Guide of Tools for Continuous Improvement and Effective Planning*. GOAL/QPC: Methuen, MA. 1994.

continuous quality improvement (CQI)

In health care, a management approach to the continuous study and improvement of the process of providing health care services to meet the needs of patients and other persons. Continuous quality improvement focuses on making an entire system's outcomes better by constantly adjusting and improving the system itself, instead of searching out and getting rid of "bad apples" (outliers).

control chart

A graphic display of data in the order in which they occur with statistically determined upper and lower limits of expected common-cause variation. A control chart is used to indicate special causes of variation, to monitor a process for maintenance, and to determine if process changes have had the desired effect.

control limit

In statistics, an expected limit of common-cause variation, sometimes referred to as either an upper or a lower control limit. Variation beyond a control limit is evidence that special causes are affecting a process. Control limits are calculated from process data and are not to be confused with engineering specifications or tolerance limits. Control limits are typically plotted on a control chart.

critical path

(1) The longest sequential series of tasks in a project. (2) Minimum necessary tasks to accomplish an objective or meet a goal. (3) In health care, a treatment protocol, based on a consensus of clinicians, that includes only those few vital components or items proved to affect patient outcomes, either by the omission or commission of the treatment or the timing of intervention.

data

Uninterpreted material, facts, or clinical observations collected during an assessment activity.

database

An organized collection of data, text, references, or pictures in a standardized format, typically stored in a computer system so that any particular item or set of items can be extracted or organized as needed.

Deming, W. Edwards

A statistics educator, consultant, and patriarch (d 1993) of total quality management who was responsible for the first sampling program in the United States used on the 1940 census. Deming taught statistical quality control to engineers and inspectors during World War II and then took the methods to Japan, where they were partially responsible for the postwar revitalization of Japanese industry.

dimensions of performance

Attributes of organizational performance that are related to organizations "doing the right things" (that is, appropriateness, availability, and efficacy) and "doing things well" (that is, continuity, effectiveness, efficiency, respect and caring, safety, and timeliness). Performance dimensions are definable, measurable, and improvable.

effectiveness

In health care, a performance dimension addressing the degree to which the care or intervention is provided in the correct manner, given the current state of knowledge, in order to achieve the desired or projected outcome for a patient. Effectiveness is not synonymous with efficiency; a consideration of cost is not required.

efficacy

(1) In health care, a performance dimension addressing the degree to which the care or intervention has been shown to accomplish the desired or projected outcome(s). (2) The extent to which a specific intervention, procedure, regimen, or service produces a beneficial result under ideal conditions. Efficacy is often used as a synonym for effectiveness in health care delivery. Efficacy is sometimes distinguished from effectiveness to mean the results of actions undertaken under ideal circumstances, the term "effectiveness" meaning the results of actions under usual or normal circumstances.

efficiency
In health care, a performance dimension addressing the relationship between the outcomes (results of care or intervention) and the resources used to deliver the care or intervention. The ultimate measure of efficiency is the cost of achieving a goal compared to the benefit achieved by the goal.

fishbone diagram
See cause-and-effect diagram.

flowchart
A pictorial summary that shows with symbols and words the steps, sequence, and relationships of the various operations involved in the performance of a function or process. A flowchart completely describes an algorithm.

force-field analysis
A method for understanding competing forces that increase or decrease the likelihood of successfully implementing change.

function
(1) A goal-directed, interrelated series of processes, such as patient assessment or patient care. (2) A quality, trait, or fact that is so related to another as to be dependent on and to vary with this other, as in *the success of the endeavor is a function of the commitment of staff to continuously improving performance and the quality of service.* (3) The actions and activities expected of a person or a thing, as in *a pharmacist's function(s) in the home care setting* or *the function of a gallbladder*.

histogram
A graphic display, using a bar graph, of the frequency of distribution of a variable. Rectangles are drawn so that their bases lie on a linear scale representing different intervals, and their heights are proportional to the frequencies of the values within each of the intervals. A bell-shaped distribution is considered normal; skewed results represent problems or inefficiencies or may signal the occurrence of unexpected processes.

hoshin planning
A planning and management technique with seven specific tools designed to help an organization target one or two "breakthrough goals," rather than trying to accomplish too many things at once.

IMS
See indicator measurement system.

IMSystem
See indicator measurement system.

indicator
(1) A quantitative measure used to measure and improve performance of functions, processes, and outcomes. (2) A statistical value that indicates the condition or direction over time of performance of a defined process or achievement of a defined outcome.

indicator measurement system (IMS, IMSystem)
A performance measurement system developed by the Joint Commission in conjunction with accredited health care organizations. It is designed to (1) continuously collect objective performance data that are derived from the application of aggregate data indicators by health care organizations; (2) aggregate, risk-adjust as necessary, and analyze the performance data on a national level; (3) provide comparative data to participating organizations for use in their internal performance improvement efforts; (4) identify patterns that may call for more focused attention by the Joint Commission at the organizational level; and (5) provide a national performance database that can serve as a resource for health services research.

information
Data that have been transformed through analysis and interpretation into a form useful for drawing conclusions and making decisions.

interrelationship digraph (ID)*
Allows a team to systematically identity, analyze, and classify the cause and-effect relationships that exist among all critical issues so that key drivers or outcomes can become the heart of an effective solution.

Ishikawa diagram
See cause-and-effect diagram.

Juran, Joseph M.
An engineer and patriarch of total quality management who is credited with the idea that although crisis management has its uses, it does not lead to quality improvement. He has written numerous books on quality, with the central theme that planning, control, and improvement lead to quality.

matrix
(1) A situation within which something else originates, develops, or is contained, as in *an organizational matrix*. (2) Pertaining to a situation within which something else originates, develops, or is contained, as in *a matrix organization*.

measure
(1) A quantitative tool or instrument, such as an indicator, used to make measurements. (2) A unit, such as an inch, specified by a measurement scale. (3) The act or process of measuring.

multivoting
A group decision-making technique designed to reduce a long list to a shorter one.

outcome
In health care, the cumulative effect at a defined point in time of performing one or more processes in the care of a patient; for example, patient survival (or death) following a health intervention is an outcome.

Pareto chart
A special form of vertical bar graph that displays information so that priorities for process improvement can be established. It displays the relative importance of all the data and is used to direct efforts toward the largest improvement opportunity by highlighting the vital few in contrast to the many others.

performance database
In health care, an organized collection of data designed primarily to provide information concerning organizational and/or practitioner performance.

performance improvement
The study and adoption of functions and processes to increase the probability of achieving desired outcomes; the third segment of a performance measurement, assessment, and improvement system.

process
An interrelated series of activities, actions, events, mechanisms, or steps that transform inputs into outputs for a particular beneficiary or customer, as in *the hospital admission process*.

process capability
The measured, built-in reproducibility or consistency of a product turned out by a process. Such a determination is made using statistical methods. The statistically determined pattern or distribution can then be compared to specification limits to decide if a process can consistently deliver a product within those parameters.

quality
(1) A character, characteristic, or property of anything that makes it good or bad, or commendable or reprehensible; the degree of excellence that a thing possesses. (2) The totality of features and characteristics of a product or service that bear on its ability to satisfy stated or implied needs. (3) Fitness for use.

* Source: Brassard M, Ritter D: *The Memory Jogger* TM II: *A Pocket Guide of Tools for Continuous Improvement and Effective Planning*. GOAL/QPC: Methuen, MA, 1994.

quality improvement
An approach to the ongoing study and improvement of the processes of providing health care services to meet the needs of patients and others.

respect and caring
In health care, a performance dimension addressing the degree to which a patient, or a designee, is involved in his or her own care decisions and to which those providing services do so with sensitivity and respect for the patient's needs, expectations, and individual differences.

radar chart*
A chart that visually shows in one graphic the sizes of the gaps between a number of both current organization performance areas and *ideal* performance areas.

run chart
A display of data in which data points are plotted as they occur over time (for example, observed weights plotted over time) to detect trends or other patterns and variations occurring over time. Run charts are capable of time-ordering analytic studies.

scatter diagram
A graphic representation of data depicting the possible relationship between two variables. A scatter diagram displays what happens to one variable when another variable changes in order to test a theory that the two variables are related. A scatter diagram cannot prove that one variable causes the other, but it does make clear whether a relationship exists and the strength of that relationship (positive, negative, zero). Also called a scattergram.

selection grid
A grid (or prioritization matrix) designed to help a team select one option out of several possibilities. It involves deciding which criteria are important and using them as a basis for reaching a decision acceptable to the group.

storyboard†
A graphic display of the methodology used and progress made by a process action team; a board specifically designated to display information related to team identification and the status of project improvement activities.

special-cause variation
The variation in performance and data that results from special causes. Special-cause variation is intermittent, unpredictable, and unstable. It is not inherently present in a system; rather, it arises from causes that are not part of the system as designed. It tends to cluster by person, place, and time, and should be eliminated by an organization if it results in undesirable outcomes.

system
A network of interdependent components that work together to try to accomplish the aim of the system, as in *a skeletal system* or *an emergency medical services system*.

task list
A list of things to be done or obtained. The purpose of a task list is to keep a team organized and on track; keep an inventory of information, tasks, or items that may be otherwise overlooked; make sure all tasks are completed; and keep an inventory of information needed for data collection.

timeliness
In health care, a performance dimension addressing the degree to which care or an intervention is provided to a patient at the most beneficial or necessary time.

** Source: Brassard M, Ritter D: *The Memory Jogger* TM II: *A Pocket Guide of Tools for Continuous Improvement and Effective Planning*. GOAL/QPC: Methuen, MA. 1994.

† Source: Air Force Quality Institute: *Process Improvement Guide*, 2nd Edition: Quality Tools for Today's Air Force, 1994.

total quality management (TQM)

A continuous quality improvement management system directed from the top, but empowering employees and focusing on systemic, not individual, employee problems.

utilization management

The planning, organizing, directing, and controlling of resource use relating to patient care by a health care organization. Utilization management programs are generally required by third-party payers, such as Medicare and Blue Cross, who may deny payment for services deemed inappropriate.

value

(1) An amount, as of goods, services, or money, considered to be a fair and suitable equivalent for something else. (2) A judgment based on the inverse relationship between the perceived quality of an organization's service and the cost of that service.

Index

Note: Page numbers followed by a *f* indicate figures; Page numbers followed by a *t* indicate tables.

A

B

C

O

P

Q

R

S

T